STORE FOOD!

BY NORMA S. LARSEN

HEN PUBLISHING COMPANY

1st Printing, June 1981
2nd Printing, September 1981

 Hen Publishing Company
P.O. Box 13112
Portland, Oregon 97213

Illustrations by Gary Larsen

Typesetting by Sherry and Dave Redford of Royal Typesetting.
Gluten recipes are printed with permission from "The Gluten Book" by LeArta Moulton
(ISBN 0-935596-11-9)

*For Gary
and
our children
with all my love*

TABLE OF CONTENTS

FOREWORD

I've become aware that basic cooking skills, common two generations ago, have become lost to "convenience." We look to others to provide what we need or want instead of doing the work ourselves. If we could no longer purchase the things we've become accustomed to, it would be to our advantage to know how to *do* for ourselves.

We live in a time of unrest and turmoil; to be self reliant could mean survival. We need to learn all we can about caring for our basic needs. "*Give* a man a fish, you feed him for a meal; *teach* him how to fish, you feed him for a lifetime."

I want to teach you how to store food and use it daily; to know how to shop economically; to prepare wholesome, nourishing foods; to be creative and substitute when necessary; to eat simple basic foods; to explore your resources in order to be financially independent; and, generally, to care for your basic physical needs. Put into practice, this knowledge should give you greater health, satisfaction and security. These hopes for you are combined in one council: Store Food!

Friends and relatives have given helpful suggestions. Special acknowledgement goes to Jane and Frank Ward, Jack and Diana Fidler, Jean Wallen, Ilena Lacaden, Gloria Johnson, Susie Davis, Pattie Paxson, Jeri Piersall and Mary Pierson.

Elizabeth Smith has given hours of skillful editing and enthusiastic support.

Most of all I want to express deep love and appreciation to my husband and family for supporting me in all good things I undertake. I have many warm memories of my husband working on the illustrations for the book.

Gary and I want to thank our best friend who gives challenge that we might grow and gives courage that we might share.

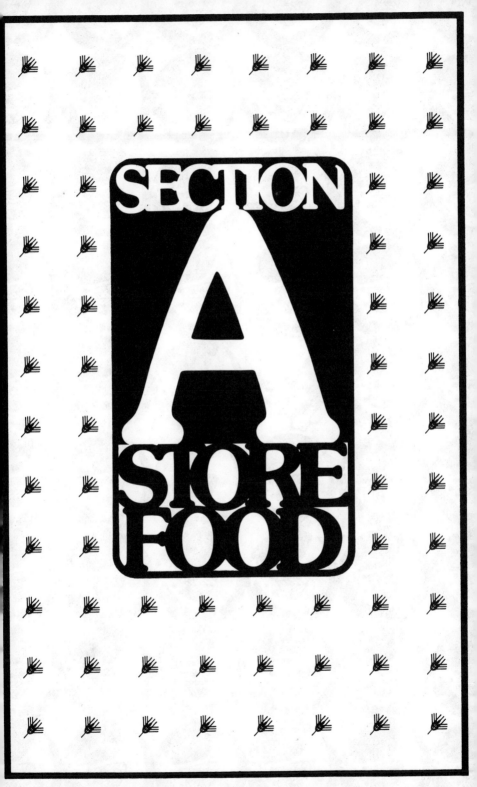

1 THE LITTLE RED HEN

I have vivid childhood memories of the story of the Little Red Hen working around the barnyard, knowing winter is coming and wanting to prepare so her family will be cozy. She says to her friends, "I have a seed of wheat, who will help me plant it?" "Not I," said the dog, "I've got cats to chase!" "Not I," said the cat, "I've got mice to catch." "Not I," said the mouse, "I've got games to play." "Then I will do it myself," said the Little Red Hen. And she did.

She weeded, watered and nourished the seed — then came the harvest — and finally it was time to grind the grain to flour and make the bread. Each time she asked the dog, cat and mouse to help but each time they had something else to do.

The great day arrived and the air was filled with the wonderful aroma of fresh hot bread. "Who will help me eat my bread?" asked the Little Red Hen. "I will!" they all eagerly replied. "No, you won't!" she said. "I have done the work while you have been too busy or played. My chicks and I will eat my bread!" And they did.

The Little Red Hen knew the principle of preparing ahead and reaping the benefit.

My husband looks at me as a Little Red Hen. Red-headed and mother of 7, I have planned ahead and reaped the benefit of storing food for the last ten years.

I'm sold on it.

We like getting the most for our money by knowing how and where to buy. We like the idea of working during time of plenty and storing for the time we need comfort and security. We like knowing we are prepared for emergency. If the stores around us close down we like the security of having developed skills to care for our basic needs.

"The plow horse does the most work, but gets the most oats and develops the strongest muscles." It is a lot of work but work having much meaning when the food is stored and the skills are developed to use it.

Unlike the Little Red Hen, I don't believe in doing everything myself. I encourage others by teaching how to obtain food storage, and how to develop skills to use it.

Most people are positive about the idea of food storage, and many are interested in planning ahead. A few considered it hoarding, and emphatically stated hoarding is wrong. I agree. Hoarding food is wrong!

The giant of Jack and the Beanstalk is an example of hoarding. He gathered as much money as he could, stashed it away — selfishly possessing it. He was determined to protect it even at the expense of another's life. This is not the intent of food storage. Food storage is planning ahead and acquiring during a time of plenty for an eventual time of need. It is using the food and replenishing it on a regular basis. It is common sense to buy wholesome, nourishing food at economical prices and to have the convenience and security of food available to prepare. In time of crisis, I would hope to share with others in need. Today, I have interest and concern for you, and hope to give you beneficial information.

Several years ago, I was a case worker for the Welfare Department. At that time my husband, daughter and I were living on the income a welfare family of three received and we were doing very well. I became aware families on my caseload were having great difficulty. Many people were on welfare because they didn't know how to use their resources. As I worked with them I understood the more skills we master, the better off we are.

This book is about developing skills.

In my seminars, the same questions are asked over and over; so in a very simple way (remember I talk with toddlers all day), I'll try to give you answers which will make storing food easy.

LET'S GET IT TOGETHER — Said the Little Red Hen, and so we shall!

2

WHY STORE FOOD

The world seems full of unrest due to catastrophies, natural disasters, labor strikes, sickness, accidents, war and inflation. In each circumstance, food storage is an effective way to provide security.

Our home is located in a lovely old area of Portland, Oregon. Large trees surround our house providing the feeling of shelter and closeness. For three years in a row, Portland was a perfect example of natural events that made food storage a wise investment.

Early in January just after midnight I was aware that my husband had gotten out of bed and was standing at the window. The aura of impending tension surrounding him told me something unusual was happening. When I reached him I could hardly believe what I was seeing. A severe storm had covered everything with inches of ice, weighing our trees down; making them creak and crackle under the enormous load.

We stood there listening to the huge branches ripping away from their trunks and crashing to the ground. As they fell upon electric wires, there were sputters and sparks. When the sun finally rose, we found ourselves in a lovely icecastle fairyland beyond description. At the same time, we were without electricity, heat, and telephone!

Because of the advance preparation, we soon had food, an alternative way of cooking and alternative heat. We gathered the family into the kitchen and played games, read books and had a good time together.

We were without conveniences for nearly a week and a half. Later, I discovered many people had been depressed and concerned because they had no facilities in their own homes; many had left to find shelter, warmth and food in school and church buildings. Many had been frightened and some even lost their lives.

Why was this a crisis for some and an adventure for others? Some were prepared!

We had ice storms two years in a row. In addition, on May 18, 1980, Mt. St. Helens erupted and literally blew its top. Ash was carried for hundreds of miles, covering some communities with up to 8 inches of fallout.

Friends of ours were visiting their family in Washington. They saw the cloud approach, like a black storm front and dump a heavy blanket of ash upon the city. Everything was dark and folks were housebound. The ash ruined the car engines if they were driven. People stayed inside to keep from inhaling the ash into their lungs. Markets closed down and customers stayed home. Our friends, fully prepared for emergency, stayed indoors and enjoyed a three day holiday with their family, just as we had during the ice storm. Those caught unprepared were fearful, uncomfortable and suffered the consequences.

The examples described lasted only a brief time; but I suggest a whole years supply of food storage. Why?

Have you ever wondered how long it would take to strip the shelves bare at the markets if there were an all-out truck and railroad strike? Or what would happen to our food supplies if war broke out? What if we had massive crop failures?

How long and how well could you live on food you have in your home and the money you have in the bank if the wage earner in your household became ill or suffered an accident? Perhaps the wage earner can only find part-time employment or needs to go to school to prepare for the future? How long could you last? A week, a month, six months?

Be prepared for a year.

A very wise person said, "If you are prepared you will not fear."

Let's say that none of the above disasters could possibly happen. We have no worry of strikes, unemployment, sickness or accident. A natural disaster would never come our way, and crop failure and war were impossibilities. Why food storage?

The best reason for having a years supply of food is beating the ever strengthening grasp of inflation. Purchasing in bulk quantity at low price saves money because food prices continue to rise.

In 1973, I remember purchasing several 60 lb. containers of honey for $9 each. The price had risen from $7 and I felt the increase to be outrageous. In 1981 when I needed more honey, the price had risen to $43 per 60 lbs.; purchasing in quantity had saved $170.

The same savings can be made on most food items.

Remember when $20 worth of groceries would more than fill the trunk of your car? Now it fits in the glove compartment!

3 WHAT TO STORE

Before getting your food storage together, let's take a look at nutrition.

To function properly, the human body needs protein. Beans, nuts, and grains contain 7 to 40 percent protein and are a very important food source. Protein is made up of 32 amino acids, 8 of which are essential and must be present simultaneously in adequate amounts to allow our bodies to manufacture the other amino acids. The essential acids are: Isoleucine, leucine, lysine, methionine, phenylalanine, threonine, tryptophan and valine. Protein from animal sources (eggs, milk, and meats) contain all 8 in sufficient quantities to be complete. Most nuts, beans and grains contain the essential amino acids but are low in one or more of them. If the correct combination of nuts, beans and grains are eaten, all amino acids are present in the body at one time and can be utilized. If animal protein (such as milk), is present at the same meal as vegetable protein (beans or grain) essential amino acids are present and the protein becomes complete. Information regarding protein is essential to preparing well balanced meals and selecting foods for storage.

THE FOUNDATION FOUR

Four basic foods could sustain life if it got right down to the nitty-gritty.

WHEAT, the hard, red turkey variety, which is less than 10% moisture and contains more than 12% protein, is an excellent storage item. It has the 8 essential amino acids but is low in lysine and needs to be combined with another vegetable or animal protein source. Stored correctly wheat will keep for years (See Ch. 7). You can make nourishing breads, cereals & casseroles from wheat. You can work flour to develop the gluten to be used as a meat substitute. You can sprout wheat, lowering the calorie count, and raising the vitamin content. Wheat can be purchased in 60 or 100 lb. bags. A grinder is essential to utilizing grain storage.

Next in importance to wheat is **POWDERED MILK**. Two types of powdered milk are available — instant and non-instant. Instant is not successfully stored longer than 6 months or so because it looses food value and changes flavor. Non-instant milk will store for years. In fact, the military uses non-instant milk all over the world. Because it is non-instant, you must beat it in a blender, whip it with a wire whisk, or make a paste (as you do with flour for gravy), to add with water. Yogurt, yoga cheese (substitute cream cheese and sour cream), buttermilk, cottage cheese, and semi-hard cheese can be made from milk storage (See Chapters 13, 17 & 18). Instant milk is usually fortified with vitamins A and D. Non-instant milk is not fortified so care should be taken to combine foods to obtain these essential vitamins. Both products are economical by comparison to fresh milk.

HONEY, the next item of the four, may be purchased in

60 lb. containers to yield maximum savings. Storing sugar as well, includes more variety for tasty things to eat. WHITE, BROWN and POWDERED SUGAR can be purchased in 50 or 100 lb. sacks. Powdered sugar substitutes can be made by whipping white sugar in the blender for 5 minutes, or until it is no longer granular. Substitutes are not exactly like commercial products but can be used successfully. Brown sugar can be substituted by adding molasses to white sugar. The amount added depends on your taste for light or dark sugar; experiment to see what you like. MOLASSES can be purchased in gallon containers and stored easily. Molasses enhances the flavor of grain and can be purchased in sealed gallon containers.

Iodized **SALT** is essential and the fourth of the foundation items. Eaten in excess, salt is harmful and contributes to health problems like high blood pressure. Used properly, it enhances the flavor of prepared food and is necessary for good health. SPICES may be purchased in the institutional sized can for savings and convenience. Often, bean and grain recipes call for ONIONS, CELERY, PARSLEY and PEPPERS. These items may be stored in powdered or dried form to be used to flavor foods when they cannot be found in fresh supply. You may dry your own in a 120-140 degree oven with the door slightly ajar, or you can use a homemade or commercially marketed food dryer. I store large quantities in air tight containers. Never throw out celery leaves. They can be chopped and left in a collander until dry. SOYSAUCE, WORCHESTERSHIRE SAUCE, BOUILLON and SOUP BASE are other items to greatly enhance the flavor of food. Don't forget VANILLA, MAPLEINE FLAVORING, and the ROOT BEER EXTRACT just for fun!

WHEAT, MILK, HONEY and SALT are the very basics. A woman told me she tried to exist on only these four foods for a whole month. In the event of a long crisis situation, she said she would rather die than eat only these four items for an extended time. That's something to think about!

What are other storable foods?

All **cereal grains** add nutrition and variety to the diet. Many vitamins exist in the outer layers of the kernel; when the whole kernel is eaten, the greatest nutrition is obtained. When the outer layers are removed, vitamins are lost.

Some of the cereal grains we enjoy include: dried corn, rice, rolled oats and wheat. Sweet corn is dried for storage and reconstituted for table use; field corn kernels are larger and are ground into meal for breads, mush, etc. Brown rice is the whole kernel and, therefore, contains the most vitamins. Converted rice is brown rice that is processed to bring the vitamins to the center of the kernel before the outer layers are polished away. White rice is the least nutritious because all the wholesome outer layers have been removed to make it light and fluffy when prepared.

OTHER FOODS TO STORE

Beans and legumes are great!

Pinto, navy, kidney beans,
California too.
Little white and yellow beans,
For us dried peas are new.
Legumes and lentils fit in here
Garbanzo, mungs as well.
Sprout them,
Cook and puree, too.
With beans you cannot fail.

That may be corny but it gets my point across! Beans are good a source of protein.

In the good old days, many families had a pot of beans

simmering on the stove most of the time. In the recipe section, you'll find ways to use beans and legumes for breakfast, lunch and dinner.

Soybeans are one of nature's miracle products! They are very nutritious and have a variety of uses. Dry, they contain 1½ times as much protein as other dry beans and are a good source of vitamins and minerals. All 8 amino acids are found in good quantity in soybeans; they can be eaten without the need of combining other vegetable protein. Soybeans are used in a variety of products including soysauce, sprouts, soy milk, mash or pulp, oil, flour, grits, protein concentrate, protein isolate, and textured vegetable protein. They are mild in flavor, and can be added to other foods without altering the flavor substantially. Ground meats, tuna fish, peanut butter and avocado are some of the foods that can be extended by adding soybeans which have been soaked, cooked and pureed.

Oil and fat are essential to the body for energy and are necessary for many kinds of cooking. Vegetable oil such as olive, cottonseed, peanut and soybean are all in liquid form; solid fats such as vegetable shortening and margarine are easily included in home storage.

Nuts and seeds need to be stored raw and whole if possible. Once roasted and/or broken they lose some food value and are more susceptible to becoming rancid. Our favorites are peanuts, almonds, filberts, walnuts, cashews, sunflower and sesame seeds. They add nutrition, flavor and texture to many recipes.

Seeds for sprouting are very important due to their high vitamin content. Sprouting in your own kitchen is included in Chapter 12. Garden seeds should be stored, also. Do you grow your own garden or have potted tomatoes in your window box in the summer? Like the Little Red Hen, have you experienced the satisfaction of working the rich earth, planting and nurturing the seed, and assisting in this miracle of nature? Gardens provide delicious fresh food, satisfying work, and opportunity for teaching lessons of life to children. Although gardening is not the subject of this book, I highly recommend growing your own edibles.

Fruits and vegetables are a must! I recommend eating fresh raw fruits and vegetables whenever possible. Fresh fruits and vegetables require underground storage such as root cellars where the cooler temperatures and higher humidity can be maintained; or basement storage rooms constructed with proper ventilation and insulation.

Freezers are a handy convenience for keeping fruits and vegetables unless we lose electric power over an extended period of time. Therefore, for storage I recommend using a variety of methods including canning or drying or purchasing commerically dried and freeze dried produce.

How about storing **canned protein** such as tuna fish, canned salmon and corned beef.

Think about items needed for **cooking and baking** such as baking soda, baking powder, corn starch, etc., they are all essential. Although baking yeast can be purchased in large #2 size cans, you can use a sour dough starter (See pg 98), instead of commercial yeast. Last of all, don't forget the **extra goodies** that make cooking easier and eating more fun. These items include jams, jellies, relishes and pickles. Commerically canned soups (cream of mushroom, celery and chicken) make sauces a snap, and commercial or home canned puree and tomato sauces are a necessity for our kitchen. I asked my husband if he thought we should store a years supply of Snickers candy bars; that idea did not receive a warm reception. (I store a 20 lb. box of carob chips though.) And how about popcorn. As a special treat we included popcorn in the storage for the children. Looking for a bargain I found the price of popcorn ranging from $27 to $34 per 100 lb. With one exception — $9.70 per 100 lbs. What a deal! I zipped to the mill, picked up my popcorn, came home and popped a kettle full. It isn't as light and kernel free as Orville's but if I use enough hot oil in my pan it's a tasty treat. Some time later I recommended this price to a friend; he told me we were eating pet pidgeon feed. But what the heck!

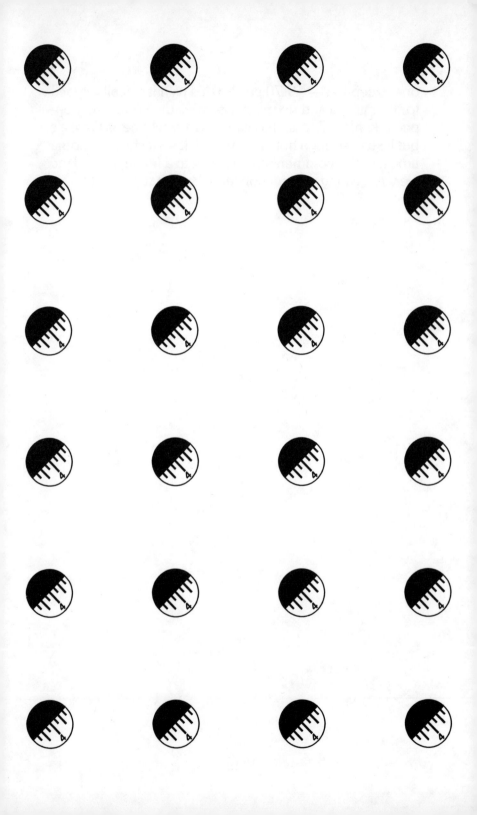

4

Think for a few minutes about the kind of food you enjoy eating. If you eat a lot of meat and few grains and beans you may feel that a vegetable protein diet will not be satisfying, nor fully nutritious. This is not true. Beans, grains, nuts and seeds are highly nutritious, easily prepared, and provide important ruffage for the body. Prepared properly they are filling and satisfying to the appetite. Vegetable proteins compliment meat and can be combined for interest and nourishment.

In the event that meat becomes too costly or unavailable, your body will be accustomed to eating whole grains and beans.

If you already know the satisfaction of eating vegetable proteins, sprouted grains and similar foods, you know the foods you like and want to purchase.

It's very important to first obtain an emergency basic foundation of wheat, milk, honey & salt, then add other foods for variety.

Take out a sheet of paper, and using the following chart, make a list of the basic foods you need. After purchasing the basics, add other nourishing foods to your storage.

Food Item	How much per Person per year	Times number in the family	Amount I need to buy
Grains: Wheat Rice Corn Others	300 lbs.	X	
Nonfat dry milk	75 lb.	X	
Sugar or Honey	60 lb.	X	
Salt	5 lb.	X	
Fat or Oil	20 lb.	X	
Dried Legumes and beans	60 lbs.	X	
Canned protein	60 lb.	X	
Fruits & Veg, canned or dried	365 lb.	X	
Garden seeds			
Water two week supply	14 Gal*	X	

The above amounts are equivalents for an average adult and provide 2300 calories per day. The chart was taken from a pamphlet titled "Food Production and Storage" by the Church of Jesus Christ of Latter Day Saints.

*14 gallons of water is a minimum amount. 56 gallons is a more convenient figure. See page 41.

CHECK LIST

☐ You are convinced you should have food storage.
☐ You know which foods are good to store.
☐ You made a list of what and how much you need.

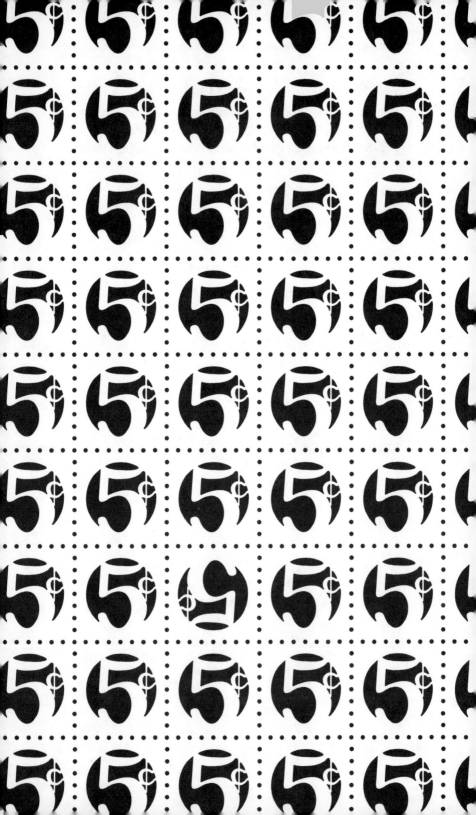

5   ECONOMY SHOPPING

Most people like to save money. Developing shopping skills places priorities in perspective and we make better purchases. The following food outlets can help to make wise and prudent shoppers of us all.

GROCERY STORES

The loss leader technique of advertising, used by grocery stores, sells an item below wholesale price in order to bring the customer into the store. Taking advantage of exceptionally good prices can save a lot if you choose wisely. When purchasing items not on sale, many stores give a 5 to 10% discount for case or bulk buying. Ask the manager about discounts.

FOOD COOPERATIVES

There are many types of cooperatives. Food Cooperatives are often small markets owned and run by a group of people. To join the group, you donate a certain number of hours selling or stocking, and are allowed to purchase at wholesale prices. If you want to purchase without donating time, you will be charged the wholesale price plus a small fee.

Other cooperatives charge a membership fee and allow you to purchase, with the group, at bulk wholesale prices.

A third is not a store but people purchasing items together in large quantities from wholesale houses. Members of the group may wish to take turns ordering and picking up the items so the responsibility does not always fall to one person.

FREIGHT DAMAGE OUTLETS

Freight damage companies buy products which cannot be sold in retail stores at regular prices because of a shipping accident. They sell the merchandise at discounted prices. Many items are unharmed and are a very thrifty buy.

CANNERY OUTLETS

Cans are heated to very high temperatures during processing. If the hot cans are exposed to cool air, they contract and can become dented. Dented and surplus cans are sold in cannery outlets. Items available may include fruits, vegetables, soups, juices, etc. Cans sold in cannery outlets and freight damage outlets are government inspected and are guaranteed returnable.

WHOLESALE HOUSES

Frequently wholesale food houses will sell to individuals purchasing bulk commodities. Call to determine house policy and prices. Near Portland we have a nut and peanut butter wholesaler who supplies all local supermarkets. Now why go to the store and pay premium prices when you could go to the source and purchase for much less? Look under "food products" in the yellow pages of your phone book for wholesale houses in your community.

BULK FOOD MARKETS

Several markets in Portland sell not only regular groceries but also carry rice, wheat, beans and sugar in 50 or 100 lb. sacks. If you buy several items at one time, they may give even greater discounts. Do you have these markets in your area? Check to see!

MILLS AND GRAINERIES

Mills and graineries are often the best place to buy wheat, rolled oats, rolled wheat, popcorn, molasses, etc. Some foods sold are intended for animal not human consumption and are not well cleaned. Be *sure* to ask. Remember to get grains high in protein and low in moisture content.

FARMS AND ORCHARDS

I home bottle fruits, vegetables, and nuts. We go right to the farm or orchard and either pick for ourselves, or purchase directly. Frequently, the farmers have dried fruits and honey available.

DAIRIES

We purchase non-instant powdered milk by 50 or 100 lb. bags from a dairy wholesale distributor. They also have powdered buttermilk, butter, and cheeses (in 5 lb. or 40 lb. blocks), purchased by the case.

NEWSPAPERS

The want ad section of the newspaper carries a section captioned "Foods and Groceries". Listed are fruits and vegetables for U-picking and other food buys. It is one way I keep informed of foods locally in season and where to buy. Another effective resource is placing your own ad in the newspaper. You might run an ad similar to this: "Wanted: fruits or vegetables for a reasonable price or free. I will pick clean." (Include your telephone number.) Fruit tree owners, having more fruit than they want to pick, may be delighted to answer your ad.

PERSONAL CONTACT

I have friends who love apple juice. For several years they passed a particular apple tree that each year went to waste. One day they stopped and asked the owner if they could pick the apples. The owner said, "Please do. We can't use all the fruit and it is such a nuisance when the hornets infest the fruit on the ground. Take all you want." Well, they cleaned the tree, the surrounding ground and bought an apple press. The tree owner was so grateful; they call my friends every year to pick the apples. My friends are delighted and have wonderful homemade cider in their freezer year round. It is delicious! and everyone benefits.

When I first started purchasing food storage, I made a list of what I wanted. I called every food outlet I could think of to find the best price. I then made a route list telling me where to go.

NOW GET OUT YOUR PHONE BOOK AND TURN TO:
1. Food Products — see what is listed and is of interest to you.

2. Grocers — wholesale and retail

24

3. Grain dealers

4. Dairies and Dairy Products — wholesale

What others can you think of?

Keep your eyes open as you travel around and you'll soon spot stores that sell in bulk. Sometimes employees in herb stores can tell you about food cooperatives. Ask people what they know about these things.

Some outlets you contact will sell in quantities larger than you can use or afford; ask friends if they would be interested in sharing a case. When we wanted to buy Baco-bits, they sold 100 lbs. for $99. Well, I didn't have $99 to spend on Baco-bits (and that's a lot of Baco-bits), so 10 of us got together and split a bag. For $10 I got two gallons of Baco-bits and paid MUCH less than I would have off the shelf.

CHECK LIST
☐ You are convinced you should have food storage.
☐ You know which foods are good to store.
☐ You made a list of what and how much you need.
☐ You know where to go for the best buys.

Now you know approximately what you need to spend. The next question needing to be answered is: How am I going to finance food storage?

6

FINANCING THE STORAGE

If your finances allow you to purchase your food storage at one time, that's great! If not, perhaps you can purchase part from your budget and do extra jobs to finance the rest. If the budget is really tight, purchase wheat and milk first. Then do extra jobs and plan a purchasing program to aid you in buying a few foods in bulk each month.

MONEY MAKING IDEAS:

Organize family work projects like RECYCLING NEWSPAPERS. One family asked their neighbors to save old newspapers. They collected the first Saturday morning of the month. Contributors put the papers on their porch, one parent drives up the street and the children collect the papers! When the car is loaded they drive to the recycling center (listed in the phonebook under recycling), weigh the load, and dump the newspapers. The car (with passengers) is weighed again, and the family is paid the difference. The price of newspaper per lb. fluctuates, but each time they collect they make enough money to purchase another food item, and it's a fun activity. Each recycling depot works differently, so call to find out the rules.

27

A family could MOW LAWNS, SHOVEL SNOW, RAKE LEAVES or SWEEP SIDEWALKS. One family WASHED WINDOWS for $50 per house, or having a CAR WASH is a fun, cooperative project.

Perhaps you could have a GARAGE SALE and clean out all the junk and treasures you have been meaning to rid yourself of. Several hundred dollars could be made this way.

If you have a second appliance or a luxury appliance that you don't really need, you might SELL it.

How about developing a TALENT that could be a moneymaker. Homemade bread, pies, and cakes sell well among neighborhood friends. Have your children leave flyers at each neighbor's door to tell them what you'll be baking on such and such a date, or, take special orders. Could you do extra sewing or make crafts? What talent do you have to bring you extra money?

One of the simplest ways to purchase food storage is to target your TAX RETURN as an investment for food storage.

How about giving and receiving storage items as GIFTS?

For Christmas last year, my parents gave our family a 40 lb. block of delicious cheddar cheese. We were delighted! I grated and froze much of it in individual quart bags; ready to use on melted cheese sandwiches, casserole dishes and cooking in general. Frozen cheese may become crumbly when thawed, but if it is grated first, it works great.

Take money out of SAVINGS. I am a big supporter of savings accounts but they are not as important as having food stored in the home.

List ideas you have.

CHECK LIST
- [ ] You are convinced you should have food storage.
- [ ] You know which foods are good to store.

☐ You made a list of what and how much you need.
☐ You know where to go for the best buys.
☐ You have a plan to finance your storage.

Okay, you have purchased your food storage and it is right there in your home and you feel exhilarated, secure and comfortable. The next step is VERY important because without it you could lose all the food you have purchased.
YOU MUST STORE THE FOOD IN PROPER CONTAINERS — IN THE PROPER WAY.

7

HOW
TO
STORE
FOOD

My most ambitious year for drying fruit came as a result of a bumper crop of sweet Italian prunes made available to us for free. I must have dried 5 or 6 bushels of them (a very commendable job), before my energy and enthusiasm sagged. As the last drier tray was emptied, I put all the fruit into plastic bags, deposited them in empty orange boxes, and sent them downstairs. I hadn't the energy to do another thing with them. School had just begun and life with the kids became more time consuming. I forgot my prunes. Around Thanksgiving, many little moths began flying about the house, especially when I was downstairs doing the wash. Being curious about their origin, I called the County Extension Division for the diagnosis: a healthy infestation of Indian Meal Moth! I was told to examine every item of food in my home in order to find the source (the eggs can reside in most foods, and can be brought home from the grocery or the mill). I groaned as I thought how much time the search would take. I had stored food for years without a problem! Searching, I told myself about the life cycle of pests — they need air, moisture and food to survive. The life cycle of the Indian Meal Moth is about 33 days, and because the egg cannot be destroyed, I had to find them as a worm or later as the moth. (The egg is usually brought in on grains, nuts, dried fruit and other food items.) It hatches on its favorite host food, spins webbing and becomes a moth. The moth can bore through light-weight plastic bags or it lands on open food and lays many eggs which hatch and begin the new life cycle. I examined their favorite foods: wheat, nuts, flour, cereals, grains, then I remembered my dried prunes and hit the pay load! Hundreds of little white, disgusting worms were crawling around feasting on my hard work!

I could have saved the food had I removed all the worms and placed the fruit in an oven at 120° for 20 minutes (no higher than 150°). But, I threw it all away only to find the worms had gotten into most of my nicely organized boxes. I had to clean half my basement. I didn't know I could have purchased a pressurized can of household insect spray and coated the surfaces and cracks of my shelving, (being careful not to contaminate the food). Instead, I paid a lot of money for a commercial company to do the job. Unfortunately, they came back three times before the moths were destroyed. A lesson well learned! From that day on I knew ALL STORAGE FOODS MUST BE KEPT IN STORAGE CONTAINERS WITH TIGHT FITTING LIDS. REMOVING EITHER THE AIR OR THE MOISTURE FROM THE CONTAINER ELIMINATES THESE PESTS AS WELL AS THEIR FRIENDS, the flour beetle, weavels, bran bugs, and who knows what else.

STORAGE CONTAINERS

Glass Pint and Quart Jars are common storage containers and can be purchased new in supermarkets, or used, in thrift stores. I wanted several dozen jars at a good price so I ran an ad in the newspaper,

"WANTED: Canning jars
Call Norma at (my number)"

To my great surprise, I had so many calls my friends got jars as benefit from the ad too. I asked the price, the number available and the condition of the jars. One woman caller impressed me — when I got to her home she had 12 dozen, clean, wide mouth quart jars with screw-on bands neatly organized and waiting for me. That was more than I had expected. When I tried to pay her she said her children were married and she canned fewer bottles and wanted to pass them on to someone who would use them. She even gave me some pint jars for good measure. (For good measure I took her a cake and I have good memories of her kindness to me.)

Glass or Plastic Gallon Jars with Screw-on Lids. Gallon quantities are often used in restaurants and hospitals; call and ask employees to save the empty containers for you. You might purchase in gallon quantities for your family and save the jars.

Five Gallon Metal or Plastic Containers with Tight Fitting Lids. Locate new containers by calling companies listed under "cans" in the yellow pages of the phone book. Fruit fillings and eggs are shipped in these containers to large commercial bakeries and can be purchased for a reduced price. Be careful to meticulously wash the used containers.

Information about **35 and 55 Gallon Storage Containers** can be obtained from can companies. Some containers have tight fitting lids with locking steel bands. Clear plastic foodliner bags which fit inside the container offer an even cleaner storage. The larger sizes are useful when storage space is limited. They can be decorated (See Chapter 11), to use with the decor of the home or they can be stored in the basement or garage, (make sure to elevate on wooden slats above concrete floors).

BATTLE AGAINST THE BUGS

Once you have adequate storage containers, the next challenge in battling against the bugs is to remove either moisture or air, or to use an insecticide. There are several methods, none of which are 100% fool-proof, but the following have been used successfully:

Moisture Removal

Testing for moisture content in wheat can be done at home. Take exactly 20 oz. of wheat from the center of a bag. Spread no deeper than 1″ in a large baking pan. Heat for 2 hours in 180° F oven. Stir occasionally. Cool completely. Reweigh. A 1 oz. loss in weight indicates about 5% moisture, 2 oz. means 10%, 3 oz. means 15%, etc.

A wonderful, granular substance, which by nature absorbs moisture, is **silica-gel**. Craft enthusiasts use the powdered form to dry flowers. Silica-gel comes in packages ranging from 1 to 8 ozs. in size, and may be purchased at craft stores or wholesale chemical companies.

For each 5 gallon container of wheat or rice, use three 6 oz. packages of Silica-gel. If the packages become damp, place them in the oven at 200 degrees for 2 hours to dry. The packet can be reused as many times as you wish.

Although unscientific, a **roll of toilet tissue** in a 5 gallon can absorbs moisture too — that's getting back to the basics!

Salt absorbs moisture and can be used by placing 2 paper bags containing ½ cup salt each, in the container (one near the top and the other at the bottom).

Air Removal

Vacuum packing is obviously the best method but it can't be done at home. Home storage experts often choose the **dry ice** method and I agree it's probably the most effective home technique. This is how it's done:

Clean and dry storage container and line with a new plastic (clear or white) bag. Don't use colored garbage bags as they emit a harmful petroleum by-product over a period of time. Place a layer of wheat in the bottom, and drop in a chunk of dry ice about 2" × 2" × 2". Fill the container with wheat and squeeze the plastic bag until nearly closed. As the dry ice evaporates it releases carbon dioxide which replaces the oxygen in the container. As the carbon dioxide is being released, the plastic bag expands (the reason for not closing the bag tightly). In 30 minutes test to see if all the dry ice is gone by completely closing the bag. If in the next 10 minutes it begins to expand, open the bag once again. The dry ice has not evaporated entirely. If the bag fails to expand, test for oxygen by lighting a match near the top of the wheat. If it goes out, oxygen is no longer present. If it burns, you need to push more dry ice into the wheat and let it evaporate. When the bag no longer expands, tie off with a twister and seal container with a tight fitting lid. Wide electrical tape can be used to seal the lid. To remove oxygen from a 55 gallon container use 2 lbs. of dry ice and follow the same procedure.

Insecticides

Diatomaceous earth is a natural product which is almost pure silica. The dust-like substance is used in toothpaste as a cleaning agent. Because it is 98% bug repellent, it is used in organic gardening as a pesticide. Combine 25 pounds of wheat (one 5 gallon can) with one cup diatomaceous earth. Mix it well by rolling the can around or by pouring the contents back and forth between containers several times. Before eating you can sieve the wheat to remove any earth, but it is not necessary.

Infestation

If you have an infestation of bugs and want to save your food you can spread it in single layers on cookie sheets, heat it to 140 degrees for 30 minutes, remove the worms and reseal it in containers. Some pest control agencies advise freezing it for 3 days. This may kill the worms but the eggs only become dormant and will hatch when returned to normal temperature.

A friend of mine who suffered infestation in TVP used Ethylene Dichloride, which he purchased in 5 liter quantity from a wholesale chemical company. He put the TVP in a 35 gallon container and placed an open baby food jar containing 2 tablespoons of the chemical on top. The lid was replaced on the 55 gallon container. Four months later (after the life cycle of the pest had passed), he opened the container, removed the chemical and used the TVP. A definite chemical odor was present when the container was first opened but soon dispelled. If you choose this method, make certain you *do not* spill the chemical on the food.

Commercial bug control for flour is done while the product is being transported in grain cars. A derivative of Chlorine gas or Bromine is put into a container on the top of the flour during transport. When the product reaches its destination the chemical plate is removed, the flour is aired, packaged and then sold to the consumer.

Electrified Wheat

Some companies package wheat in heavy protective bags which are ready for storage without treatment by the consumer. The wheat has been treated by electricity (hence the name "electrified wheat"), or by very high heat. The bags, however, are susceptible to rodents.

HOW TO STORE SPECIFIC ITEMS

All foods should be used and rotated (except air tight freeze dried foods or any food which has been treated with cobalt. Either is reported to store indefinitely). It is extremely important to replenish food supplies as they are used. All food storage should be kept in a cool, dark, dry area. (Not resting directly upon concrete flooring.)

Grains, rice, pasta products, dry corn, rolled oats and wheat:
Treat for moisture or air and seal in air-tight containers.

Beans, legumes and soybeans: Store in air-tight containers.

Powdered milk: It can remain in original purchase bags, unless rodents could be a problem, then store in plastic bag inside an air-tight container.

Salt: Store in air-tight container.

Honey: Store in original container. Honey will become granular but can be melted down using a very low heat (so you don't make candy).

Sugars: Store in original sacks unless moisture is a problem (moisture makes it hard). Then store in air-tight containers. An apple slice added to brown sugar keeps it soft.

Spices: Purchase them in cans or bottles, not in packages. Keep lid on tight.

Oils: Light, moisture, air and warmth contribute to turning oils and fats rancid. If oil is bought in quantity and small quantities are used at a time, transfer to smaller containers, filling them right to the top to eliminate air. Seal with a tight-fitting lid. Oils keep about 9 months.

Shortening: Store in original containers. Shelf life is about 15 months.

Margarine: Can be purchased by the case and frozen or kept in the refrigerator for 8 months.

Nuts: Store in air-tight containers. The less done to nuts, the longer the shelf life. Whole, raw nuts, in the shell, keep the longest.

Seeds: For sprouting purposes seeds must be stored moisture free in air-tight containers.

Fruits and vegetables: Canned or home bottled, store in cardboard boxes separating the glass jars with cardboard dividers. Dry fruits and vegetables need to be stored in air-tight containers. Dried fruits are one of the favorite foods of many pests.

Canned protein: May remain in case boxes or may be stored on sturdy shelving.

Cooking and baking needs: Must remain dry. The original boxes can be stored in larger air-tight containers.

Extra goodies: Store glass jars in boxes with cardboard dividers. Store popcorn and carob chips in air-tight containers.

Eggs: See Chapter 15.

STORAGE PRECAUTIONS AGAINST NATURAL DISASTERS

A natural disaster could cause great damage to stored foods.

For example, during an earthquake, weight on shelving can cause the shelves to rip from the wall and collapse on the floor. Glass and plastic containers stored on shelves are often lost because of breakage. Shelving is practical for short term convenience but the bulk of food storage should be stored in the following way.

1. Canning jars should be kept in boxes with cardboard dividers and stacked no more than three high.

2. Plastic and metal 5 gallon containers should be stacked only three high as they will break or suffer damage if dropped more than four feet. 35 and 55 gallon containers may rupture when dropped.

5, 35, and 55 gallon enamel coated steel containers are nearly indestructable and can withstand nearly any disaster. They are also animal proof.

8 WATER STORAGE

Man can live much longer without food than he can survive without water, so a two week emergency water storage is essential. A larger storage is required if you store freeze dried foods. When an earthquake occurs, only a small number of people die at the time of the quake. Many survivors die later due to polluted water and adverse sanitary conditions.

HOW MUCH WATER SHOULD YOU STORE AND HOW DO YOU STORE IT?

The emergency sanitation guidelines published by the Oregon Emergency Services Division recommends:

Drinking	3 pints
Cooking	2 quarts
Personal hygiene	1 gallon
Laundry and dishwashing	2 gallons
Total	.4 gallons per person, per day

Multiply the number of persons in your family × 4 gallons

× 2 weeks to find the quantity to be stored. Use clean containers, adding 2 drops of chlorine bleach per gallon. Store in a dark place so algae does not grow. If taste is a consideration, replace the water every six months.

Containers

Any watertight container can be used except those that rust or corrode. The best containers are 55 gallon enamel coated, steel drums, with a spicket. They hold a lot, take a minimum storage space, and are nearly indestructible. (Check the yellow pages under "cans.")

Most hospitals, clinics and laboratories use cardboard, cube-shaped containers that hold 19 liters of saline water. The containers are easily stacked and have plastic bags on the inside, complete with spicket for easy use. Call the hospital or the lab and ask if an employee would set aside discarded containers to be picked up once or twice a week. They are excellent for water storage.

Your water bed is another place to store a large amount of water. Use only for personal hygiene as poisonous chemicals are included to inhibit the growth of algae.

AFTER A DISASTER

If an emergency or natural disaster occurs, immediately shut off the water supply to your home. Locate the turn off valve *before* you need it. If you can't find it, use a wrench to shut off the water outside at the meter. Second, turn off the main gas valve at the hot water tank or disconnect the electric heating element and close the valve on the tank inlet. Open the hot water tap and allow the water to pour from the tank drain. Once collected, allow the water to stand until the sediment drops to the bottom. Disinfect before drinking.

There is water in the pipes of your home. Shut off the

water supply, turn on the faucet in the highest room, (allowing air into the plumbing system), and draw water from the lowest faucet in the house. The water in the top tank of the toilet is also usable.

To Disinfect Water

Boil the water briskly for 5 minutes. Allow the water to cool and store in sterile, covered containers. If the taste is flat, pour the water back and forth from one clean container to another allowing air to be absorbed. This is the safest and simplest method to treat water in your home.

Chlorine. You can use ordinary household bleach to disinfect (5.25% available chlorine). Add 5 drops of bleach for each gallon of clear water. Stir well and let stand for 30 minutes. The water should taste faintly of chlorine; if not, add more bleach.

Iodine. Use ordinary household tincture of iodine (2% iodine and 2.4% sodium iodine). Add 8 drops of iodine for each gallon of clear water. For muddy or mossy water, use 15 to 25 drops of iodine for each gallon of water. Stir well and allow to stand for 30 minutes. Again, the water should have a distinct medicinal taste. If not, add more iodine.

Water purification tablets can be purchased from pharmacies or sporting goods stores. Follow directions on package.

There are many **water purifying units** on the market. Some use filters that must be stored and replaced. Others are carbon bonded to silver and do not need replaceable filters. Make sure the unit purifies polluted as well as municipally treated water.

Reservoir water, contaminated with radioactive material, should not be used until it has been cleared by the State Health Division Department of Radiation Control. Chlorination and boiling do not remove radioactive particles. Water storage is essential for survival in this situation.

43

Sanitation

What if the toilets don't work?

You can use one of the 5 gallon storage cans to construct a toilet. Make a seat by using cleats on the underside of a regular flush toilet seat (this prevents the seat from sliding about), or make your own seat. Put one gallon of water and ⅓ gallon of chlorinated bleach in the bottom of the can. When the can is full of waste, empty into an operating sewer, or bury the contents, making sure it is well covered with at least 12″ of tamped earth. Thoroughly clean the can with soap and hot water and disinfect every time the contents are emptied. Chlorine products may be used for disinfecting purposes.

HOME GARBAGE DISPOSAL

Separate your household garbage into three groups:

1. All garbage that will spoil and decay should be kept in the house in a water proof, rodent proof container and never kept more than 4 days. Dig a burial hole 2′ × 2′ × 3′ deep. If it is possible, empty the garbage into the hole every day. Cover it with at least 6 inches of tamped earth. When the hole is filled to within a foot of the ground surface, fill the remaining space with earth and tamp thoroughly.

2. For non-combustible refuse (bottles, tin cans, etc.), store them in boxes or other containers in an open area until they can be collected. All items should be well cleaned. Tin cans should be opened at both ends and smashed flat.

3. Combustible refuse (papers, cartons, etc.), may be burned unless there is danger of the fire spreading, or that gas lines may have been damaged during the disaster. A 50 gallon drum or similar container makes a good home incinerator.

OTHER STORAGE ITEMS

In addition to food and water several other things should be stored.

If you cannot heat your home, you should have enough bedding to keep everyone warm.

A years supply of clothing or equivalent fabric and sewing supplies are necessary, as well as first aid and cleaning supplies.

You should store enough fuel (wood, coal, matches, etc.), to heat a portion of your house for 1 year. If it is not possible, store at least enough fuel for cooking purposes.

9 RECORD KEEPING

I recommend keeping two kinds of records.

1. A memory file. Whenever you purchase, record the item, date, place (including address and phone number), the price, and quantity purchased. If the item was fruit I picked and later canned, I also include bottles yielded. This file tells me where to go for the best buys each year.

2. Keep track of the inventory so your storage never gets too low. Hang a paper and pencil near your storage and mark it whenever you add to or take something away. You can immediately see which items need restocking. It will also indicate what and how much of a particular item you have used.

10

NO STORAGE SPACE

I frequently hear, "But I don't have the room to store food." I guess it depends on what you think is important. Most people have never been without food for any length of time. I suggest folks fast (totally, without food or water) for two days and see if they can't find some space for food storage.

It is ideal to have a fruit and storage room in your home or garage that is insulated so the temperature stays at 45 degrees F., or below. It is best if the storage place is dark, cool, and dry. Short term shelving is handy and makes it more convenient to use storage items. However, storing almost any place is better than not storing at all. One family with limited storage space decided it was more important to have food than to have bed frames, so they placed their box springs on many 5 gallon containers filled with wheat, beans, milk, etc. Others use large 35 and 55 gallon containers as end tables in their living rooms. The containers may be covered with fabric, reflective mylar, contact paper, or painted. Lamps or plants can be placed on a large container draped with a tablecloth. How about stacking boxes and containers (3 high) against one whole wall.

A floor to ceiling drape can be hung on a track to cover the containers.

CHECK LIST

- [ ] You are convinced you should have food storage.
- [ ] You know which foods are good to store.
- [ ] You made a list of what and how much you need.
- [ ] You know where to go for the best buys.
- [ ] You have a plan to finance your storage.
- [ ] You bought your storage and brought it home.
- [ ] You stored it in the right kind of containers and processed it correctly.
- [ ] You stored water.
- [ ] You are keeping records.
- [ ] You arranged an area for food storage.

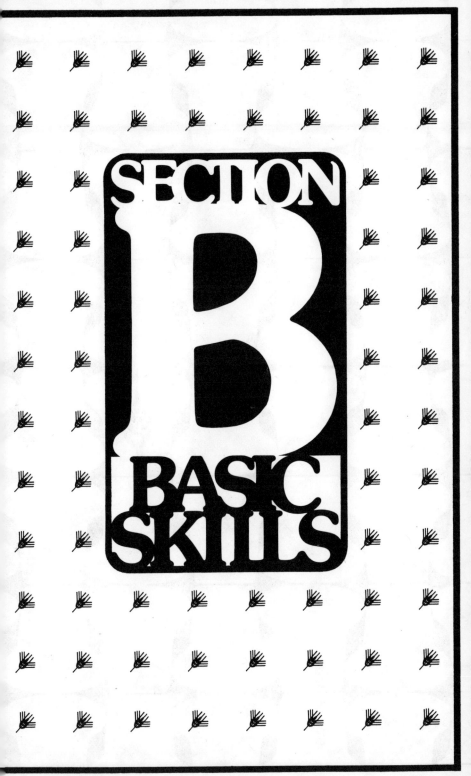

SECTION B
BASIC SKILLS

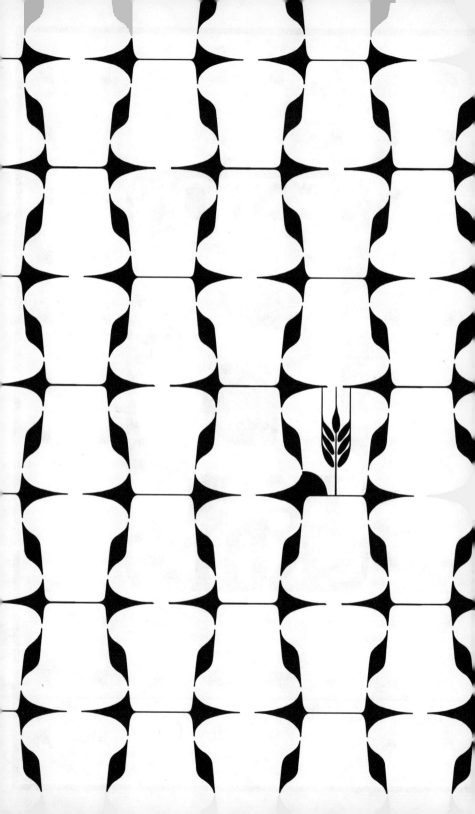

11 & BREAD MAKING GRAIN MILLS

For centuries the basic food and mainstay of civilization has been bread. Whether eaten as unleavened bread, yeast loaves, tortillas, or crackers it provides excellent nutrition for the growth and function of the human body. Bread plays an important role in the food storage diet.

Successful bread making is a skill acquired with experience. With knowledge of the bread making process, a few bread making experiences, and careful observation, you will soon make delicious and beautiful bread.

INGREDIENTS AND SKILL

Leavening Agent

Yeast is the living organism that causes bread to rise by the process of fermentation. Granular yeast is first dissolved in warm water (85 to 90 degrees F). Water temperatures above 90° kill the fermenting action of the yeast and conversely, water that is too cool fails to activate the yeast. Add a *little* sugar and it speeds the action. Stirring the yeast or adding *too* much sugar (or salt) retards the action. As the yeast begins to ferment carbon dioxide gas is formed. The gas bubbles are trapped in an elastic framework made by gluten. As the bread is worked and kneaded the elastic quality of the gluten is developed further and consequently the trapped carbon dioxide makes the bread rise.

Baking powder and soda are leavening agents frequently used with quick bread, cakes and pancakes.

Liquids used in the bread dough

Using water to moisten the dough yields bread with an open grain and crisp crust. It is used in making French and Italian bread. Milk produces a nourishing bread with a velvety grain and brown crust. Breads made with milk retain moisture. Vegetable or potato water increases moisture and volume while producing a coarser grain. Before baking, I check the refrigerator for leftovers (cereal, canned fruits, vegetables, etc.) and add them to the liquid. Adding leftovers makes moist bread with a coarse texture and they are not noticed in the final product.

Sugar

Sugar (although not too much) helps the yeast manufacture leavening gas. It adds flavor and aids in browning.

Salt

Add salt to give flavor and to control fermentation.

Shortening

Add shortening to give a finer texture to the bread and crust. It preserves the bread.

Flour

Rye, oats, bran and cornmeal flour do not contain gluten and must be used in combination with wheat flour when making yeast bread. The gluten traps gas bubbles allowing bread to rise. The gluten is developed by mixing, pounding and kneading.

Flour varies in nutritional value depending on the quality of the original grain, on the amount of heat present as it was ground, and the length of storage time from grinding until the bread is made and eaten. The most nutritious breads are made from grains high in protein and from flour ground without heat. Heat destroys vitamins! Consider this fact when choosing a grain grinder.

Kneading

Kneading is mixing and blending dough by hand that is too stiff to mix with a spoon. Flour your hands and flatten the dough on a lightly floured surface. Pick up the edge of the dough farthest from you and fold it toward you. With the heel of your hand press and push the dough away from you. Turn the dough a quarter of the way around and continue lifting, folding, pressing and pushing until the dough becomes smooth and elastic (approximately 10 minutes).

After kneading, place the dough in a greased bowl and cover with a warm damp cloth. Allow the dough to sit in a warm place free from draft until enough gas has been produced to double the original size of the dough. Turn onto a floured board. Knead 2 minutes and shape into loaves. Cover the loaves with a clean cloth and allow bread to rise the second time. Bake according to instructions on recipe. Bread is finished baking when it shrinks slightly from the side of the pan and sounds hollow when tapped.

Hand kneading machines are effective and quite inexpensive.

Electric bread kneaders can be purchased in many different styles.

Batter breads have a soft dough and the gluten can be developed with an electric hand mixer.

Biscuits and muffins should be kneaded only enough to mix the dough. The batter should remain lumpy for the lightest results.

Storing Bread

Homemade bread can be baked in quantity and stored in the freezer for approximately 3 months.

Remove freshly baked loaves from pans and completely cool on racks or clean toweling to prevent condensation. To retain moisture while cooling, cover bread with toweling. Store in plastic bread wrappers.

Fresh bread should be stored at room temperature except when weather is hot and sticky — then refrigerate.

Reheat frozen bread by placing thawed loaf in a brown paper bag. Saturate bag with water and bake in 400 degree oven for 10-15 minutes.

Stale bread can be sliced and dried to make zwieback (good for teething children, pie crusts, croutons, etc.). My grandmother hung a bag of zwieback near the back of her old wood cooking stove. Zwieback was a tasty after-school snack or was floated in soups. Banana or pumpkin bread can be dried for a delicious treat. Zwieback can be stored for weeks unrefrigerated.

SECRETS FOR MAKING GREAT BREAD

Perfect bread has nice shape, light texture, even color and is moist and tasty.

Problem	Explanation	Solution
Distorted shape	1. Loaf raises too long and collapses	1. Raise only until dough retains finger print when pressed.
	2. Insufficient raising	2. See #1
	3. Air bubble in loaf	3. When forming loaf, press out bubbles.
Too Heavy	1. Liquid too cold/hot	1. Liquid should be 85-90 degrees.
	2. Too much oil or sugar.	2. Decrease amount.
Dry & Coarse	1. Too much yeast	1. Decrease yeast.
	2. Too much flour	2. Decrease flour.
	3. Too long rising in pan	3. Raise only until double & retains imprints of finger when pressed.
	4. Insufficient kneading	4. Knead longer time.
Dark streaks	1. Too much flour added during kneading.	1. Add flour before kneading.
	2. Insufficient kneading	2. Knead more thoroughly.
	3. Oiling surface too heavily before first rising period	3. Turn dough over in an oiled bowl to coat surface.
Crust too Brown	1. Too much sugar for baking temperature	1. Decrease sugar.
	2. Oven too hot.	2. Lower temperature
	3. Too long baking time	3. Decrease baking time.
	4. Crust over exposed	4. Midway through baking cover with foil.

GRAIN MILLS

Today's market offers a variety of electric grinders. Factors worth considering when choosing a grain grinder are: Does the grinder have a variety of settings ranging from very fine for making cake flour to coarse grind for making cereals? Do the grinder parts need replacing very often? Is it easy to clean? In the event of a power shortage, can an electric grinder be converted to a hand grinder? Can a hand grinder be attached to a bicycle for easier grinding?

Electric grinders fall into three basic types. Because **Slow Operating Grinders** grind slowly, the flour stays cool and the nutritional quality remains. On the average, they grind 4 lbs. of wheat in 22 minutes. If you lack patience, this grinder provides the opportunity to develop it. For persons who plan ahead, they work just fine.

Fast Operating Grinders grind 4 pounds of wheat in 9 minutes but the powerful motor heats up and some vitamins are lost although much less than in commercial flour.

A mill that works on the principle of **Micronization** explodes the grain. It works very fast and remains cool, but only produces the finer flour for bread making. A second mill is needed to grind cereal.

Be aware commercial flour is ground fast, processed, bagged, and shipped to stores for purchase. All fresh homeground flour is more nutritious than commercial flour.

Slow and fast grinding mills use either stone or steel burrs.

Stone Burrs remain cooler than steel but they eventually wear out and need to be replaced. Occasionally grit might get into the flour. Stone burrs also gum up if peanuts or soybeans are ground. They function best with wheat and corn.

Steel Burrs get hot but never have to be replaced. If they become dull, they can be sharpened. They also grind a greater variety of grains and nuts.

Unfortunately, there is no perfect choice; select carefully to suit your needs.

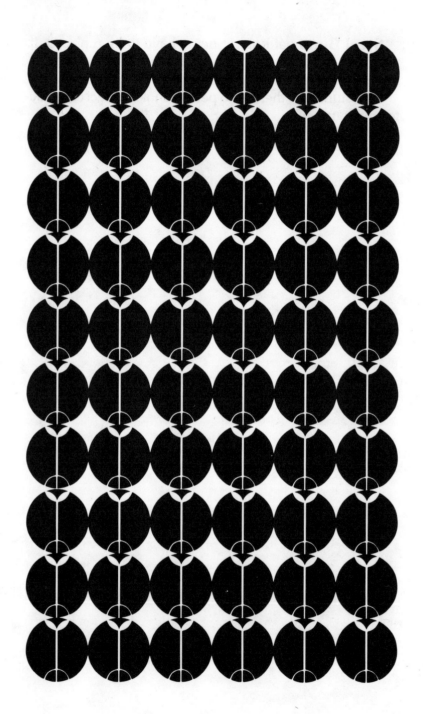

12 SPROUTING

Let me give you an example of why I think sprouting is so important. Beans, seeds, grain and nuts are very nutritious foods. When they are sprouted they dramatically increase their food value. The nutritional content of oat sprouts was tested at an Eastern University. The test determined sprouted oats contained 50% more biotin, nicotinic acid had increased 500%, pyridoxine (B6) 500%, pantothenic acid 200%, folic acid 600%, thiamine (B1) 10%, inositol 100%, and vitamin B2 1350%. Other tests have shown after 5 days Vitamin C in soybeans increased 553%, niacin in mung beans increased 400% and Riboflavin in wheat, barley and corn increased 400%.

Seeds contain fats and carbohydrates. If harvested at the proper time, the fats and carbohydrates are changed to vitamins, sugars and proteins. This means sprouts are less fattening, while being more nutritious and digestible.

When seeds are sprouted the food potential can increase 10 fold. For example: one unit fenugreek seeds planted yields approximately 350 units of seed. If we stopped the cycle there, we would benefit. However, if the 350 units of seed are sprouted the yield is approximately

3000 units of sprouts. Think how many additional people could be fed if we sprouted grain.

Once we know how to sprout, we have a garden at our fingertips.

Any unhulled, whole seed, bean, grain or nut can be sprouted with the exception of potato and tomato seeds which are toxic. Sprouts most commonly used are: alfalfa, cress, fenugreek, garbanzo, mung bean, mustard, lentil, radish, soybean and wheat. When purchasing seeds, be sure to buy those *not* treated with fungicides, mercury or other poisons. Store in a cool, dry, dark area (not resting directly on concrete).

HOW TO SPROUT

Preparing:

After consulting the yield column on the following chart, measure the seeds. Soak overnight in lukewarm water (1 cup seed to 4 cups water; except when using gelatinous method). After soaking, drain the water (saving it for bread making or soup stock).

METHODS OF SPROUTING

Jar Method

Presoak seeds in a jar large enough to contain sprouts. Cover the opening with a piece of cheesecloth, netting or nylon stocking, secured with an elastic band. A piece of fiberglass screening may be cut to fit the opening and secured with a screw-on band. This method provides an easy way to rinse and drain the seeds. Prop the jar at an angle to allow for constant drainage during the germination process. Keep the seeds in a warm, dark place where air can circulate around them. Try propping the jar in a square tray and covering with an open, upside-down grocery bag. Keep the seeds moist by rinsing (the following chart indicates frequency). When sprouts have grown to the desired length, the chlorophyll content can be increased by placing the sprouts in indirect or artificial light until the leaves turn green.

Rack Method

You will need a tray, for catching the moisture, a rack, and paper toweling. Presoak seeds. Place the rack in the tray and cover with a double-thick layer of paper toweling which has been soaked in water. Sprinkle the presoaked seeds evenly over the toweling. Cover the seeds with another double-thick layer of moist toweling. Place the tray in a large plastic bag and put the whole thing in a dark cupboard. Make sure the end of the bag is open so the air can circulate. Water seeds by removing top layer of paper toweling, dipping it in water, squeezing out the excess and replacing over the seeds. They must be kept moist but not wet. When the desired length is obtained, (see chart) increase the chlorophyll by removing the tray from the bag and placing the sprouts in indirect or artificial light until the leaves turn green.

Gelatinous Method

This method is used for Chia, Garden Cress and Buckwheat that become jelly-like when they come in contact with water. Use a large saucer from a terra cotta flower pot, a larger shallow container (to be used as holding tray), and aluminum foil. Cover saucer with water and boil 5 minutes to eliminate unwanted bacteria. Soak saucer several hours in clean water. Measure equal amounts of seeds and water. Fill saucer with water, sprinkle surface with seeds, and let stand until water is absorbed. (Seeds will have formed a solid jelly-like mass.) Place saucer in shallow container. Fill lower container with water to the rim of the saucer. Replace water as terra cotta saucer absorbs moisture. Cover saucer lightly with aluminum foil, allowing moisture and air in while keeping light out. When sprouts reach desired length, remove foil and "green" in indirect or artificial light.

The chart on page 65 gives details for seeds you might want to sprout.

7 Day Garden

Wheat, buckwheat, sunflower seeds, lentils and garden cress can be grown in a 7 day garden. The young plant is allowed to grow until the first leaves open. This increases bulk and chlorophyll content and yields more vitamin C.

How to do it:

Find a sturdy box which is 2-3" deep. Seal it using plastic wrap or aluminum foil. Spread 1" of good soil over the bottom.

Soak seeds in water overnight. Spread evenly one layer deep over moist soil. In order to retain moisture, cover with 8 layers of wet newspaper. Place in a plastic bag in a warm, dark place.

When seeds have germinated and begin pushing up against the paper, (usually about 3 days) remove the bag and wet papers. Put the sprouts in the sunlight and sprinkle lightly 2 or 3 times daily.

When the first leaves are fully open, harvest by cutting with scissors just above the soil.

Use in salads, garnish or blend in drinks.

SPROUTS

	Method	Temperat. in degrees	Rinse × pr day	Harvest length	Sprouting time	Yield
Alfalfa	jar	68-86	two	1½-2" greened or ⅛ inch	3 to 5 days (24 hrs for ⅛")	3 T seed = 1 qt. green sprouts ¼c = 1½c ⅛" sprouts
Almonds	rack	68-86	2-3	when root = ⅛" to ¼"	3 or 4 days	½c = ¾c sprouts
Barley	jar	70-80	2-3	when root = length of seed	3 or 4 days	½c = 1c sprouts
Beans: Black Great northern beans Fava Haricot Kidney Lima Navy Pinto Red & Windsor	jar	68-86	3-4	1" to 2"	3 to 5 days	1c = 4c sprouts
Buckwheat	gelatinous	68-86	one	when root = ¼ - ½"	2 to 3 days	1c = 3c sprouts
Chia Seeds	gelatinous	68-86	one	1" - 1½" greened or ⅛" ungreened	4 days - greened 24 hrs - ⅛" sprouts	2T = 3 to 4c 1½" sprouts ¼c = 1c ⅛" sprouts
Corn	jar	72-68	2-3	½" root	2 to 3 days	1c = 2c sprouts
Garden Cress	gelatinous	50-68	two	1½" greened	3 or 4 days	1T seed = 1½c sprouts
Fenugreek	jar	68-86	1-2	3" greened	4 to 5 days	¼c = 4c sprouts
Flax Seeds	jar	68-78	2-3	1 to 2" greened	about 4 days	2T = 1½ to 2c sprouts
Lentils	jar	68-86	2-3	about 1"	3 to 4 days	1c = 6c sprouts
Millet	jar	70-80	2-3	¼" root	3 to 4 days	1c = 2c sprouts
Mung beans	jar	68-86	3-4	About 2"	3 to 4 days	1c = 4 - 5c sprouts
Oats	rack	70-80	one	when root = length of seed	about 3 days	1½c = 2c sprouts
Pumpkin seeds	jar	68-86	2-3	¼" root	about 3 days	1c = 1c sprouts
Rice	jar	50-80	2-3	when root is length of seed	3 or 4 days	1c = 2½c sprouts
Rye	jar	50-68	2-3	when root is length of seed	3 or 4 days	1c = 3½c sprouts
Sesame	jar	68-80	4 or more	when root is length of seed	about 3 days	1c = 1½c sprouts
Soy beans	jar	68-86	every 3 hrs	2"	about 4 days	1c = 4 to 5c sprouts
Sunflower seeds	jar	65-75	two	root no longer than seed	24 to 36 hours	1c = 3c sprouts
Vegetable Seeds Cabbage Chinese Cabbage Cauliflower Collards Kale Brocolli Brussel sprouts Kohlrobi Mustard Turnips Beets Chard Endive Lettuce Radish	jar	68-86	two	1 - 2" greened	3 to 5 days	varies with seed 1T makes 1 to 2 cups
Wheat	jar	70-80	2-3	when roots are about ½"	about 3 to 4 days	1c = 3½ to 4c sprouts

13 MAKING YOGURT

Years ago, I remember reading an article in the newspaper about a group of people who had been discovered living high in the mountains of Eastern Europe. These people were unusual because they lived to be well over a hundred years old and had healthy, vigorous and happy lives. A simple lifestyle, hard physical labor and fresh air contributed to their longevity. They were being studied because their diet appeared to be the primary reason for their good health. They ate mostly fresh fruits, vegetables, grains, and much yogurt.

We've eaten a lot of yogurt since then. Yogurt has a variety of uses and a fresh, pleasant taste. It is very beneficial to the human digestive tract (I give it to the kids to treat diarrhea) and it is very easy and inexpensive to make.

HOW TO MAKE YOGURT

Method 1: Used when the milk product has been heated to 190° F during processing, including: instant or non-instant powdered milk, canned milk, sweetened condensed milk, etc. Best results and longer storage life are obtained if all the containers and utensils are sterilized by boiling (or steaming) in water for 5 minutes.

1. Add 3 cups non-instant powdered milk or 4¾ cups instant powdered milk to one gallon of water, which is 110° F. (For one quart, add warm water to ¾ cup non-instant or 1¼ cup instant milk powder). Make thicker yogurt by increasing proportion of milk powder to water. If you do not have a thermometer use the baby bottle test. Put a little on your wrist. If you can't feel it, the temperature is fine.

2. Add starter, 1 cup per gallon or 3 Tbs. per quart and mix. Plain yogurt purchased from the grocery will serve as the first starter. (Reserve 1 cup as a start for your next batch.)

3. Incubate 2 to 8 hours at 110 to 120 degrees F. Don't let the temperature get higher than 120 degrees as it will kill the bacterial action of the yogurt starter.

There are many ways to incubate yogurt. Place it in a food dryer, in a gas oven using the heat from the pilot light, in a picnic cooler containing hot water, or in a commercial yogurt maker. You can wrap it in a thermal blanket or do anything that will maintain 110 to 120 degree temperature. It is very important not to disturb or jiggle the yogurt during incubation as that causes a separation of water (whey).

4. Store in refrigerator after yogurt has thickened. Chill several hours before serving. When homemade yogurt is cut into, there will be a separation of the whey. Pour it off, absorb it with a paper towel or stir it in, making the yogurt thinner.

Method 2: To be used when milk product has not been heated to 190° F during processing (any fresh milk).

1. Heat milk to 190 - 210° F. This destroys undesireable organisms which prevent coagulation.

2. Cool milk to 110 to 115° F. Proceed as in Method 1, number 2.

Yogurt can be used in every course of a meal with fresh and healthful results. Fruit and vegetable yogurt drinks and frozen yogurt are delicious. Yogurt adds zest and coolness to cold summer soups, fruit salads, and serves as salad dressing and topping. Serve it plain at the table and let everyone add their own favorite fruit and sweetener.

Sour cream or cream cheese can be substituted by yoga cheese containing a little salt and sugar.

Yoga Cheese is made from yogurt by placing a layer of paper toweling in a colander which is set in a larger bowl for draining purposes. Pour yogurt into colander and cover with two more layers of paper toweling. Allow to drain in the refrigerator for several hours. When whey is drained away the remaining yogurt thickens. Add salt and sugar to taste and use it as a spread for crackers, in dips, or as toppings.

As my 4 year old says "Yogurt is Yummy."

SECRETS FOR MAKING GREAT YOGURT

Problem	Explanation	Solution
Not Thickened	1. Not adding enough starter.	1. 3 TB per quart 1 c per gal.
	2. Temp. of milk too hot or cold.	2. Add starter between 110-117° F.
	3. Disturbed or jiggled	3. Do not disturb.
	4. Temp. to hot or cool during incubation.	4. 105-120° incubation temperature.
	5. Starter dead.	5. Use unpasteurized starter.
Runny and Thin	1. Not enough dry milk.	1. Increase dry milk.
Too Much Whey	1. Disturbed or jiggled.	1. Do not disturb.
Flavor too Tart	1. Milk too warm when starter added.	1. Add starter at 110°.
	2. Incubation period too long.	2. Reduce time.

14

MAKING GLUTEN

If you are a meat lover, read on. Someone once said, "What you can do with meat, you can do with wheat!" Gluten is the protein portion of the wheat grain and is valuable as a meat substitute. When separated from the starch and bran, it becomes a stretchy, elastic-like substance that may be used for added protein in the diet. It can be flavored as meat, or sweetened and used as dessert. Using gluten takes work and some skill, but it is rewarding to know how to use this protein substitute effectively.

HOW TO MAKE GLUTEN

7 cups very warm water
14 cups whole wheat flour
Mix ingredients together forming a moist dough. (If using an electric breadmixer, knead for 10 minutes. If working by hand, knead vigorously, or pound with meat hammer for 10 to 15 minutes.) Pinch off handfuls, flatten like pancakes, and soak one hour in warm water. Fill a large bowl ⅔ full with warm water, knead each handful in the water until all the starch and bran falls away. You will be

71

left with a very fiberous substance. Place it in another bowl and continue washing the remaining patties. When all patties are washed, fill the second bowl with clear water and knead patties again briefly. When finished with the washing process you'll have 2 to 5 cups of raw gluten (depending upon the protein content of the wheat). After the wash water has settled, you will notice three distinct layers. The top layer is water containing vitamins and minerals useful for making breads, soups, etc. The next is starch, which may be dried and used as baby or face powder, or as a thickener (like cornstarch). The bottom layer contains coarse bran and when dried can be used as bran cereal or in bran muffins, etc.

GLUTEN STEAKS

Fill a 32 oz. greased tin can to ½ full with raw gluten. Cover, to 1″ above the gluten, with a well seasoned ham, beef or chicken bouillon broth. Lift gluten allowing the broth to coat the sides and bottom of can. Bake at 325 degrees from 2 to 4 hours or until the water is nearly absorbed. The gluten should have a firm texture and spring back to the touch. Shake the gluten out of the can and slice ¼″ rounds. Dip the slices in milk or beaten egg and coat with bread or cracker crumbs. Fry in a small amount of oil until browned on all sides. Serve with sauce or gravy. Freezes well.

GLUTEN ROAST

Shape raw gluten as you would bread by tucking in sides and ends. Place in pot with tight fitting lid. Cover with a broth well seasoned with bouillon, soy sauce, onion flakes, etc. Bake, covered, at 250 degrees for 8 to 9 hours until the moisture is absorbed. Do not allow it to dry out. Slice for serving; or slice, cube, or grind it for use in other recipes. Freezes well.

GROUND GLUTEN

After the raw gluten has been washed, let it rest for 5 minutes. Place on well greased cookie sheet. Pat and stretch until ½" thick. Bake in a 350 degree oven for 15 minutes, turn and bake an additional 15 minutes. During baking time, bubbles may appear — puncture with fork. After baking, fold the warm gluten several times and place in a plastic bag to distribute moisture. Set aside for several minutes. Tear off pieces and grind with a meat grinder using a medium disc. Proceed as with ground beef.

Recipes for sausage balls and patties, gluten parmesan and gluten in various sauces can be found in Chapter 16.

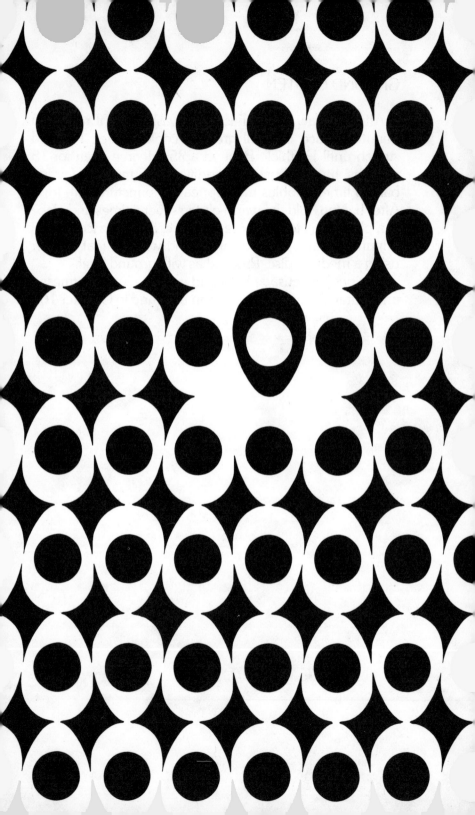

15

STORING
EGGS

Because an egg is designed to house an unborn chick, the shell is porous enough to allow oxygen in and to let gases out. The membrane protects it from harmful bacteria and mold. The shell protects the egg, for a short period of time, when kept cool. Within one or two weeks, both the white and yolk begin to lose firmness and become watery. To store eggs for an extended time, you must seal the pores of the shell.

In the good old days, eggs were preserved in many ways; rubbing them with grease, submerging them in salt, and by a successful process termed **"waterglassing."** Fresh eggs (less than 12 hours old) were submerged in a syrupy solution of sodium silicate and water. This chemical is used today to seal pipes, concrete flooring and as an adhesive in the paper industry. Waterglassed eggs cannot be boiled because the shells become soft. The egg whites cannot be beaten stiff, but the eggs can be used for baking purposes or for scrambled eggs. I located the chemical "waterglass" by checking the yellow pages under "chemicals."

Dipping the eggs in **paraffin** is an effective technique *if* the eggs are very fresh. Allow two pounds of paraffin to cover 3000 eggs. When processed by this method they can be stored for a couple of years.

Freezing is an excellent way to keep eggs but impractical during electrical power failures.

Powdered eggs — Call commercial bakeries to find where they can be purchased in your area. Dried eggs can be used for nearly all baking needs.

GELATIN SUBSTITUTE FOR EGGS

If egg storage is not practical, and fresh eggs are not available, gelatin can be substituted for eggs needed in baking. While it does not have the same nutritional value (one egg has 6 grams of protein, while 1 tsp gelatin has 2½ grams protein), it has only 9 calories per teaspoon as opposed to 70 calories per egg. Gelatin also stores well and is easily available.

Recipe for Gelatin Substitute (equivalents)

1 egg = 1 tsp gelatin + 3 Tb cold water + 7 tsp boiling water

2 eggs = 2 tsp gelatin + ⅓ c cold water + ½c boiling water

3 eggs = 1 Tb gelatin + ½ c cold water + ½c boiling water

Place cold water in a mixing bowl.
Sprinkle in the gelatin to soften.
Mix thoroughly with spoon.
Add boiling water and stir until dissolved.
Chill (preferably in freezer) until thick.

Beat gelatin with mixer until frothy (Follow this step exactly!)
Add to recipe in place of eggs.

16 MAKING TOFU

Tofu is a soft, nutritious soybean product used by all oriental and Eastern cultures. It has a variety of names depending on the locale.

Tofu has been used for centuries as a meat substitute because it provides excellent protein.

Tradition tells us early Mohammed priests (devout vegetarians) ate tofu, and it is used by vegetarians today.

Tofu is made from complete soybean protein. An 8 oz. serving of tofu is the protein equivalent to 2 eggs, 1⅔ c milk, or a 3¼ oz. steak, and the calcium content of tofu is comparable to cow's milk.

Tofu is easily digestible and is fed to babies, elderly folks, and people recovering from surgery.

Tofu may be served alone or used as an extender with other foods as the taste is mild and blends well with stronger flavors.

FIRST MAKE SOY MILK

Wash 1 cup soybeans and soak them overnight in 6 cups cold water. Using 1 quart water to one cup beans, liquify in the blender until smooth. Strain puree through a fine-mesh cheesecloth or a clean dishtowel. The result is soy milk. The soy pulp (mash) left in the towel can be used as an extender in recipes or combined with spices for a sandwich spread.

Bring soy milk to a boil and proceed with one of the following methods:

First Method

Boil milk for 3 minutes.
Turn off heat.
Dissolve 1 rounded Tb Epsom salts in ¼c warm water.
Add this mixture slowly to the soy milk while stirring gently.
Let stand for 5-10 minutes. (It will curdle during this time.)
Strain curds in colander lined with cheesecloth.
Rinse with cool water.
Store (covered in water) in air-tight container up to 4 days.

Second Method

Place 3 cups soy milk in double boiler, bring to boil.
Add ½ tsp Citric Acid and mix slowly.
Turn off heat, allow to cool in double boiler.
Strain curds in cheesecloth-lined colander.
Cover with water, store in refrigerator in air-tight container.

WAYS TO USE TOFU

Cube and add to clear soups.
Make a pattie with two parts tofu and one part mashed potato, season, fry.
Scramble like eggs, season.
Mix with tuna, gluten, or hamburger and shape in patties.

Mix with rice in a casserole — add other interesting foods and condiments.
Stuff dates or prunes, mixing with fine coconut.
Mix with mayonnaise and crushed dill seed for sandwich filling.

17

MAKING COTTAGE CHEESE

Making cottage cheese is a skill that was common several years ago. Our grandmothers made it regularly from skim milk left after making butter. The same process is used today with much success.

Ingredients and Utensils Needed:
1 gallon milk
activator (yogurt, buttermilk or rennet tablet)
casserole dish, enamel pan or other flat container (not aluminum)
pan larger than the bottom of your dish (to make double boiler)
spatula or wide blade knife
dairy thermometer
long handled spoon
cheesecloth
colander

CLABBERING THE MILK

Make one gallon milk by adding 3 cups non-instant or

4¾ cups instant milk powder to warm water. (Fresh milk works too.) Add one of the following to clabber:

1 cup unflavored fresh yogurt

1 cup cultured buttermilk

¼ rennet tablet (dissolved in ½ cup cold water)

Mix the milk and activator together and cover it loosely with a towel to let air in but keep dust out. Place in warm spot (75-85 degrees F) for 6 to 18 hours. Clabbering occurs when milk thickens and pulls away from the sides of your bowl as you gently tip it. The whey rises to the top.

CUTTING THE CURD

The curd is cut to allow the whey to separate from the solid milk. Carefully cut the curd in 2″ parallel lines starting at the top and drawing the knife or spatula toward you. Turn the bowl 90 degrees and do the same again. Now you want to make cubes, so place your spatula at sharp angles following the original cuts and undercut the curd. You should have 2″ cubes when done. If you cut too much, more whey than necessary will be released and the curd will become rubbery, so take care with this step.

HEATING THE CURD

Using the double boiler technique, place your bowl in a larger pan containing a few inches of water. Insert a dairy thermometer into the curd and slowly heat to 115 degrees F, stirring carefully every few minutes. Do not break the curd. Maintain this temperature for about 30 minutes, being careful not to let it go higher as the curds will become tough and dry. The curds will settle to the bottom of the bowl.

STRAINING THE CURD

Line a colander with cheesecloth, place the colander in a larger bowl, and gently pour in the curds and whey. The whey can be used in a casserole or other cooking as it has important minerals and B vitamins. After most of the whey has drained off, take the four corners of the cheesecloth containing the curds, tie it, and hang from the faucet until the dripping has stopped.

STORING AND EATING

If you intend to freeze the cottage cheese, do not rinse. Pack into containers and freeze. Rinsing the cottage cheese minimizes the acid flavor. If you plan to eat it within a few days, rinse, add a little cream, salt or seasoning, and serve chilled. Dill, chives, and parsley are tasty seasonings. One gallon of milk yields approximately 1½ pounds of cottage cheese.

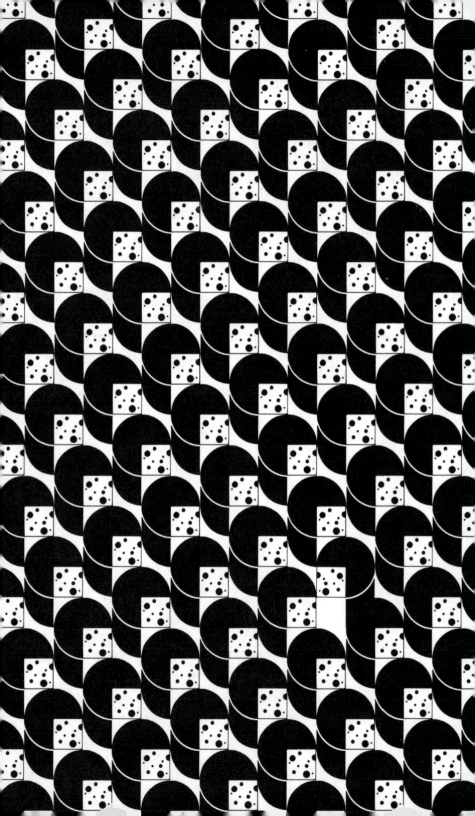

18 MAKING CHEESE

Cheese making has long been an exclusive art, but if you are patient and follow directions exactly, you may succeed in making a variety of delicious cheeses.

Raw or pasturized whole milk are usually used in cheesemaking. Instant or non-instant milk can be used, but the flavor of the finished cheese will not be as rich as commercial cheese.

Plan on making at least three to five pounds at a time — anything smaller tends to dry out too much in the aging process. (The following recipe makes approx. 3½ lbs.) Make sure all the utensils and bowls are washed well in hot soapy water and thoroughly rinsed in very hot water. They must be scrupulously clean! Plan to spend 4½ hours making cheese.

Ingredients and Equipment Needed:
    milk (4 gallons)
    buttermilk (1 cup)
    rennet tablets (1 tablet)
    salt (2½-3 Tbs.)
    kettle (large enough to hold above recipe)

dairy thermometer
long spatula or wide blade knife
long handled spoon
4 pieces of cheesecloth (20″ × 20″) or similar material
colander or large container
a cheese hoop, clean dish towel or other non-stretch
    fabric
safety pins
2   8″ round cake pans
paraffin and brush

MAKING BUTTERMILK — FOR CHEESE MAKING AND OTHER USES

The milk needs to be innoculated with a lactabacillus culture so other types of bacteria won't grow during the aging process and ruin the cheese. Buttermilk contains lactabacillus bacteria. Use 1 cup commercial buttermilk for this recipe, or prepare your own culture as follows: Purchase 1 quart commercial buttermilk and divide evenly into 4 clean, scalded quart jars. Fill jars with milk, stir well, seal with lids and allow to sit at room temperature for at least 4 hours. You now have 4 quarts of cultured buttermilk for making cheese, drinking or for use in other recipes. Repeat this process by adding buttermilk saved from the last batch to more milk.

RIPENING THE MILK

Get the biggest enamel or stainless-steel canning kettle you can find. Do not use aluminum. Combine milk and buttermilk. Over a low flame, heat the milk to 86 to 90° F and let the milk ripen by allowing it to sit for 1 to 2 hours. (The milk can sit for up to 12 hours.) Do not let it stand in direct sunlight.

MAKING THE CURD

Dissolve 1 rennet tablet (for every 4 gallons of milk) in ½ cup cold water. Using a dairy thermometer, heat the milk to 86 to 90°. Turn off heat. Add the rennet. Stir well for one minute, cover and let it rest for 35-60 minutes to clabber milk. Test the curd by sticking a clean finger into the mixture at an angle and lifting it out slowly. If the curd breaks "clean" over your finger, the curd is ready for cutting. If it doesn't break clean — be patient until it firms up. Cut the curd with a long spatula or knife in parallel lines ½ inch apart. Turn the container 90 degrees and cut perpendicular to the first cuts. You want to make cubes, so place your spatula at sharp right angles following the original cuts and undercut the curd. Undercut in several directions until you think the curd is well divided.

HEATING THE CURD

Place the curd on very low heat. Careful, if it's too hot it will scorch the curd on the bottom of the kettle. (If you have a kettle still larger than the one housing the curd, place a little water in the bottom and use it as a double boiler.) Heat curd to 105° stirring every 3 to 5 minutes. As it heats, the curd shrinks and whey is formed. Pour or dip off the whey (save it for bread making or pour it on your garden). Add salt. Using a long handled spoon or a clean hand, carefully stir the curd to mix the salt. The curd will have become quite firm by now.

PRESSING THE CURD

Place the clean cheesecloth in a colander or a large, clean container that is at least the same volume as the curd. Pour the curd into the cheesecloth and bring up the corners of the cloth to form a ball. Twist and squeeze out as much whey as you can. Hang and let drain for at least 15 minutes, preferably until cold. Remove ball of curd from cloth and place in a clean piece of cheesecloth. To form cheese wheel, place curd in a cheese hoop (if you have one) and apply 50 lbs. of weight. If you don't have a cheese hoop, take a clean dishtowel, fold it several times making a long band about 4″ wide. Wrap the band around the middle of the ball of curd as tightly as possible and fasten with safety pins. Put the ball on a clean towel which has been placed in the bottom of an 8″ shallow pan, forming the bottom of your cheese wheel. Place another flat pan on cheese and pile about 50 lbs of weight on top. Allow it to stand overnight. (You can make a more sophisticated cheese press with some ingenuity.) Smaller heads of cheese need less weight. The weight presses the individual curd into a solid piece of cheese. Remove weights and cheese hoop or 4″ band. Place cheese on a rack so air can circulate. Cover with toweling and let dry at room temperature for 2 to 3 days. Turn twice daily and wipe with cloth dipped in vinegar or rub with salt.

AGING

Your cheese may be eaten at this stage. Wrap it in plastic wrap and place in refrigerator for at least 3 days before serving.

You may want to snitch a little taste but if you want aged cheese — be patient. You must wait for at least 60 days. Wipe off the outer surface of the cheese wheel and tightly wrap it in a double layer of cheesecloth. Using caution, melt one or two pounds of paraffin (no higher than 100 degrees). Brush the melted wax over the entire surface of the cheese or dip portions of the wheel in the wax until the entire surface is coated. Date the cheese so you will know when it is properly ripened. Store in a cool, dry place and turn once every few days. If you notice mold under the paraffin, don't worry. If the cheese begins to swell, you are in trouble. It indicates the milk wasn't ripened properly. In 60-90 days your cheese is properly aged and you may eat it. (Remember, the older it is, the sharper the flavor.) Various herbs and natural coloring can be added to the milk after it has ripened to produce other flavors in the cheese.

Sources for Rennet:

Dairy Laboratories
2300 Locust Street
Philadelphia, PA 19103

Marshall Dairy Laboratory
14 Proudfit Street
Madison, WI 53703

Christian Hansen's Laboratory
9015 West Maple Street
Milwaukee, WI 53214

NOTES

SECTION

C

RECIPES

19

BREADS

Since the beginning of civilization, bread has been the mainstay of good eating.

Whole Wheat Bread

2 Tbs dry yeast
½ c warm water
2 Tbs sugar or honey

White Bread

3 Tbs dry yeast
1 c warm water
1 Tbs sugar or honey

Sprinkle yeast over sweetened water and brew for 5 minutes until bubbly.

5 c hot tap water, vegetable, whey
  or gluten water
2 Tbs salt
⅔ c oil
⅔ c honey, white or brown sugar
3 Tbs molasses (opt)
12 to 15 c freshly ground whole
  wheat flour

4 c warm milk
2 c warm water
2 Tbs salt
⅔ c oil
½ c sugar
15 c white flour (approx.)

Blend liquid, salt, oil, sweetener and 7 cups of flour with electric mixer for 5 minutes. Add yeast mixture and remaining flour (one cup at a time) beating with spoon after each addition. Add only enough flour to make firm dough (not sticky). Turn onto a floured board, knead until smooth and elastic (about 5 minutes). If you are not using an electric mixer, stir in flour with a large spoon and knead the dough for 10 minutes. Place dough in oiled bowl, turn once, cover with a warm damp cloth, let rise until doubled in bulk (about 1 hour). Punch down and form into loaves.

1. Conventional loaf: Pressing out air bubbles, mold the dough into loaf shape. Place seam side down into greased loaf pans.
2. Cylinder loaf: Drop dough into well-greased 32 oz. juice can until ⅔ full. Press down.
3. Braided loaf: For each loaf, divide dough into 3 parts. Roll each into a 10″ rope. Pinch 3 pieces together at one end, braid and pinch together at finish. Fold under ends and place in greased loaf pan.
4. Cinnamon loaf: Roll dough into 9″ × 12″ rectangles. Spread with margarine, sugar, cinnamon, nuts, and raisins. Beginning on the long side, roll tightly, sealing ends by pinching together. Place the loaves seam side down in well greased loaf pans.
5. Round loaves: Shape the dough into balls and place on greased cookie sheets.
6. Scones: Pinch off a handful of dough and flatten, fry in oil until golden. Serve with jam or honey.

For all loaves (not scones), cover with a warm damp towel and let rise until doubled. Bake at 350° for 45 minutes.

For dinner rolls, hamburger buns, hot dog buns, or sweet rolls, double the sweetener, yeast, shortening, and add an egg. If milk is the moistening agent, texture will be finer. Roll out dough, cut into desired shape, and place on greased baking sheets. Raise until doubled (about 2 hours for rolls). Bake at 400° for 15 to 25 minutes or until done.

Before baking, I take all the leftovers from the fridge, warm and add them to my water before adding the flour. (The above recipes can take about 2 extra cups.) It prevents wasting food, adds moisture to the bread and no one even knows the "extras" are there.

Unleavened Bread

1¾ c flour	**½ tsp salt**
1 c water	

Mix lightly with a spoon. For a substantial, crisp, cracker-like bread, spread the rough dough ⅛″ thick on greased cookie sheet. Prick with a fork. Bake at 350° about 15 minutes or until done. Can be brushed with milk and topped with sesame seeds, etc.

Corn Bread

The following is an authentic cornbread recipe straight from "Midge" — truly a Southern Belle.

1 c white flour	**1 c yellow corn meal**
¼ c sugar	**2 eggs**
3 tsp baking powder	**1 c milk or buttermilk**
1 tsp salt	**⅓ c soft shortening**

Sift flour with sugar, baking powder and salt; stir in corn meal. Add eggs, milk and shortening. Mix just until smooth (about 1 minute). Do not overbeat. Pour into greased 8″ square pan. Bake in 400° oven 20 to 25 minutes.

English Muffins

1 Tbs yeast	4 Tbs sugar
¼ c warm water	3 Tbs shortening
1 c warm milk	1 egg
1½ tsp salt	4½ whole wheat flour (approx)

Sprinkle yeast over water, let brew 5 minutes. Combine milk, salt, sugar, shortening. Add 2 cups flour & beat well. Add yeast, egg & remaining flour. Knead well, let rise until doubled. Roll ¼" thick. Cut with No. 2½ size can. Place biscuits on cornmeal or coarse flour to rise until doubled. Bake slowly on heavy *ungreased* griddle or fry pan at 375°. Bake 7-8 minutes on each side. Yield 1 dozen 4" muffins.

English Muffins with Raisins

To the above recipe add:

½ c raisins	¼ tsp nutmeg
1 tsp cinnamon	2 Tbs honey

Follow above directions.

Arabian Pocket Bread

2½ c warm water	1½ tsp salt
2 Tbs yeast	3 Tbs oil
1 tsp sugar	6 c flour

Mix ingredients in order given until the flour is combined. Knead ONLY until smooth. Place in a covered bowl and let rise until double (1½ hour). Punch down and knead a few times. Divide into 16 equal parts and roll out into small 4" to 5" rounds. Place on greased or cornmeal sprinkled cookie sheets. Let rise 30 to 60 minutes. Heat oven to 500°. With rack in lowest position, bake 5 minutes. They are best when fresh. Cut the pocket bread in half crosswise and fill it with sandwich spreads, sprouts, refried beans, casseroles, etc.

Irish Soda Bread

4 c whole wheat flour	2 tsp soda
2 c white flour	2 tsp baking powder
½ c brown sugar	3 c buttermilk (or milk +
2 Tbs salt	3 Tbs vinegar
	to make 3 cups)
	4 Tbs oil or margarine

In a bowl combine first 6 ingredients. Add buttermilk, oil and beat until batter is blended but lumpy. Fold in 1½ cups raisins (optional). Spoon batter into 2 greased and floured 8" round cake pans, do not smooth surface. Bake at 425° for 30 minutes or until an inserted toothpick comes out clean. Turn onto wire rack. Serve warm, cooled, or sliced and toasted.

Dilly Bean Bread

2 Tbs dry yeast	1 tsp salt
2 c warm water	4 tsp dried dill weed
3 Tbs sugar	7 to 8 c flour
2 c pureed beans (soak, cook	1 beaten egg
and puree pinto or great	2 tsp salt
northern beans)	2 tsp dried parsley
4 Tbs instant minced onion flakes	4 Tbs parmesan cheese
4 Tbs oil	

Sprinkle yeast over water and sugar. Let stand 15 minutes. Combine beans, onions, oil, salt and dill weed. Mix well. Add yeast to bean mixture. Stir in flour to make stiff dough. Turn onto floured board, knead until smooth and elastic. Put in oiled bowl, let rise until doubled. Punch down, shape into loaves (2) and place in greased pans. On top make several ½" deep diagonal slashes. Brush with beaten egg. Combine salt, cheese and parsley and sprinkle over loaf. Cover and let rise until doubled. Bake 350°, 40 minutes.

Dilly Cheese Bread

2 Tbs yeast	2 tsp salt
½ c warm water	1 tsp soda
2 c cottage cheese	2 unbeaten eggs
at room temperature	4 c flour
4 Tbs sugar	
2 Tbs instant minced onion flakes	
2 Tbs margarine	
4 Tbs dill seed	

Soften yeast in warm water. Combine cottage cheese, sugar, onion, butter, dill, salt, soda and eggs. Mix by hand until well blended. Add flour. (Dough should be stiff but slightly sticky.) Let rise 50 to 60 minutes. Stir down. Place in center of greased cookie sheet or in a loaf pan. Let rise til doubled. Bake at 350° 40 to 50 minutes. Serve hot.

Sour Dough Starter

2 c warm water	2 tsp honey
preferably potato water	
2 c flour	

Mix well. Put in uncovered bottle. Allow mixture to ferment in a warm room for 5 days, stirring several times a day to aerate batter. Mixture will smell yeasty and bubbles will appear. After using starter, replace with equal amounts of water and flour. Refrigerate unused portion in a glass jar with tight fitting lid. Shake frequently. Before using again, activate by adding 3 Tbs each of flour and water. Stir.

Sourdough Bread

1½ c starter
2½ c lukewarm water
  (can be half milk, half
  water)
2 Tbs sugar

1 Tbs salt
3 c white or whole wheat
  flour
¼ c oil
5 c whole wheat flour

Place starter in a large bowl, add water, sugar, white flour, salt, beat until smooth. Let stand at room temperature 12 to 15 hours (overnight) lightly covered. Stir down, add oil and blend in wheat flour. Knead until smooth on lightly floured board. Dough will feel slightly sticky. Divide in half, shape into loaves (be sure to work out air pockets). Place in greased 9″ × 5″ × 2″ pans. Cover. Place in oven and let rise for 2 to 5 hours until dough is 1″ above pan sides. Bake 375° for 45 to 50 minutes. Turn onto wire racks. Brush with oil.

Corn Tortillas

2⅓ c masa harina   1½ c warm water

Mix flour and warm water. Using hands, shape dough into smooth ball. Divide dough into 12 equal sized pieces, roll until very thin and round. Place one at a time on a preheated, ungreased, medium-hot griddle or in a heavy frying pan over medium high heat. Bake, turning frequently until the tortilla looks dry and is lightly flecked with brown specks (about 1½ to 2 minutes). Keep it soft. Serve warm, or cool and wrap airtight for storage in refrigerator or freezer. To serve, reheat quickly on a hot griddle.

Flour Tortillas

2 c flour   ¼ c shortening
1 tsp salt   ½ c lukewarm water

Mix flour and salt. Add shortening. With pastry blender cut shortening until particles are fine. Gradually adding water, mix with fork to make stiff dough. Form a ball and knead on lightly floured board until smooth and flecked with air bubbles. Oil surface of dough, cover tightly and refrigerate for up to 24 hours. Dough handles easier after being refrigerated and returned to room temperature. Divide dough into 10 balls. Roll out paper thin. Bake on very hot ungreased griddle until freckled - about 20 seconds on each side. Heating tortillas too long makes them brittle. Immediately put them into an air tight dish and keep warm in the oven until all tortillas are heated. Serve warm, topped with refried beans, spicy tomato sauce, sprouts, cottage or semisoft cheese.

Pumpkin Bread

5 cups flour
4 tsp soda
4 c sugar
1 tsp cloves
1 Tbs salt

1 large can pumpkin
1 c oil
1½ c raisins
2 c chopped nuts

Combine ingredients well. Pour into 3 well greased loaf pans. Bake 350° for 45 to 60 minutes or until an inserted toothpick comes out clean.

Bran Muffins

1 c whole wheat flour
1 tsp soda
1½ c bran
½-¾ c raisins

1 beaten egg
½ c honey or molasses
¾ c milk
2 Tbs shortening

Blend dry ingredients. Add egg & raisins. Moisten with remaining ingredients. Stir slightly to blend. Bake 20-30 minutes at 400°.

Popovers

2 eggs
1 c milk

1 c whole wheat flour
½ tsp salt
1 Tbs oil

Beat eggs in bowl. Add milk, flour & salt. Beat 1½ minutes with electric beater. Add oil & beat ½ minute (overbeating reduces volume). Fill 6-8 well greased preheated muffin tins to ½ full. Bake in hot preheated oven 475° for 15 minutes. Reduce heat to 350° & bake 25 minutes until brown & firm. Serve warm or stuff with salad or sandwich filling.

Make ahead mixes are time savers. Store in air tight containers in a cool, dry place or in the refrigerator. Date and use within 3 months.

White Mix

11 c white flour
5 Tbs baking powder
2 Tbs salt
1 c non instant milk
2 c shortening

Wheat Mix

6 c whole wheat flour
3 c white flour
2 c non instant milk
1 Tbs salt
1 c sugar
¼ c baking powder
2 c vegetable shortening

Cornmeal Mix

4 c white flour
4 c cornmeal
1½ c dry milk
½ c sugar
¼ c baking powder
1 Tbs salt
1 c shortening

Oat Mix

6 c white flour
¼ c baking powder
1 Tbs salt
1½ c dry milk
1½ c shortening
2 c rolled oats

Combine dry ingredients. Cut in shortening until mixture is crumbly. Store. For Oat mix, add oats last. Stir.

Pizza Crust

1 c white or cornmeal mix
¼ c water

Stir until soft dough is formed. Knead for 30 seconds. Shape into ball and roll into circle 12" in diameter. Place on greased baking sheet. Brush with 1 Tbs oil and top with spicy tomato sauce (page 125), ground gluten sausage (page 127), parmesan cheese.

Scottish Scones

2 c white mix
1 beaten egg
⅓ c water

½ tsp lemon extract
½ c raisins

Combine all ingredients. Knead 30 seconds on lightly floured board. Divide dough in two equal parts. Pat or roll each in circle ½" thick. With sharp knife, cut circle into 6 triangles. Place on greased baking sheet. Brush tops with milk and sprinkle with sugar. Bake at 450° for 10 to 12 minutes. Makes 1 dozen.

Wheat Muffins

3 c wheat mix
2½ Tbs sugar

1 slightly beaten egg
1 c water

Combine wheat mix and sugar. Add egg and water all at once. Stir until moistened and batter is lumpy. Fill well greased muffin tins ⅔ full. Bake at 400° for 15 to 20 minutes. Makes 12.

Cornmeal Muffins

3 c cornmeal mix
1 beaten egg

⅔ c water

Add egg and water to cornmeal mix. Stir just enough to moisten. Fill greased muffin tins ⅔ full. Bake 400° for 20 to 25 minutes.

Oatmeal Biscuits

2 c oat mix   **4 Tbs water**

Combine mix and water with fork. Knead dough 30 times on lightly floured board. Roll to ½" thickness. Cut with floured cutter. Place biscuits on greased pan and bake at 425° for 8 to 10 minutes. Makes 10 biscuits.

Oatmeal Dumplings

2 c oat mix   **1 c water**

Thoroughly combine mix and water. Spoon onto boiling stew. Cover and boil gently 12 minutes without removing cover.

Applesauce Oat Loaf

3 c oat mix   **1 c applesauce**
1 c brown sugar   **½ c water**
½ c raisins   **1 egg**

Combine ingredients until well blended. Pour batter into greased loaf pan. Bake at 350° for about 1 hour.

Homemade Noodles

2 c white or whole wheat flour   **2 eggs**
3 to 6 Tbs water

Place flour in a large bowl and make a well in center. Break eggs into well, and beat lightly with fork. Using a circular motion, draw flour from sides of well while adding water — 1 Tbs at a time. Continue mixing until all flour is moistened. When dough becomes stiff, use hands to finish mixing. Knead dough 10 minutes. Invert bowl over dough and let rest 30 minutes. Divide dough into 4 parts. Work one portion at a time. Cover remaining dough. On floured board, roll dough into 8 × 12" rectangle, 1/16" thick. If dough becomes sticky, flour both sides. Place rectangle on lightly floured board; let rest and dry (approximately 5 minutes), turn once. Dough should have the feel and flexibility of soft leather. (If extra time is needed, cover with plastic wrap.) Noodles become brittle when dried too long.

Starting at narrow end, roll each rectangle (jelly-roll fashion) cut in ¼″ strips. Unroll and hang noodles on wooden dowel or lay on floured board to dry (30 minutes). Don't let them become brittle. (After drying, store in a plastic bag in refrigerator for 2 days or freeze. Will keep about a month.) To cook, drop noodles in 4 quarts boiling water to which 1 Tbs salt and oil have been added. Stir gently with a fork. Cook, uncovered 2 to 3 minutes. Drain and serve. (Don't thaw frozen noodles before cooking.) Yield: 4   1 cup servings.

20 BREAKFAST

Ground wheat, rice and corn give variety to hot cereal making. Grind fine for gruel, medium for mush and coarse for porridge; or cook wheat or rice whole.

Don't forget rolled wheat and rolled oats for hot and cold cereal.

Basic recipe: 1 quart boiling water
½ tsp salt

Gruel
1½ c finely ground wheat, corn or rice. Add slowly to boiling water using a whisk. Cook for 3 minutes.

Mush
1½ c medium or coarse ground wheat, corn, rice, rolled oats, rolled wheat or any combination. Slowly add to boiling water using a whisk. A double boiler can be used for wheat, corn & rice. Cook 15 to 30 minutes or until soft.

Porridge
2 c rice "or"
2¼ c whole wheat
Add to boiling water, cover. Simmer rice about 45 minutes. Bake wheat 5 hours at 150° - 200°
OR
Add wheat or rice to boiling water in thermos. Let sit overnight. In the morning it is ready.

Serve with: Milk and honey, brown or white sugar, cinnamon and
             nutmeg.
             Margarine or peanut butter.
             Chopped dry or canned fruit with milk.
             Sweetened yogurt.
             Toasted sunflower seeds and milk.
             Sprinkle a little powdered milk instead of sugar. Milk
             contains lactose or milk sugar and adds sweetness. Add
             reconstituted milk.
             Rice is good with butter and soysauce, salt and pepper or
             milk, cinnamon and sugar.

Leftovers: Add to water when making bread
             Make scrapple

Scrapple:

Pack a greased loaf pan with warm left over cooked cereal (cornmeal
is frequently used). Refrigerate. The next morning, remove from pan,
slice thinly, dip in flour and fry in hot fat until brown on both sides.
Serve with syrup, sorghum molasses, jam, fruit or sweetened yogurt.
Add 1 tsp sausage flavoring (page 127) to every cup cooked cereal for
variety.

Cold Cereals

Raw oats

Try raw rolled wheat or oats (they absorb stomach juices and keep you feeling full for
hours). — don't overdo — grains expand and could cause severe discomfort if *too* much
is eaten.

Put raw rolled oats or wheat in a bowl. Top with chopped, dried or canned fruit.
Sprinkle with nuts. Serve with milk, sugar or honey.

Mussili

Soak 2½ cups rolled oats in 2 cups pineapple juice or milk overnight. In the morning add
chopped apples, prunes, raisins or dates. Sprinkle with chopped nuts.

Grape Nuts

2 c unbleached flour
2 tsp salt
2 tsp baking powder
1 c brown sugar
2 c whole wheat flour

2 c yellow corn meal
2 c rolled oats
1 c molasses
2 c milk

Sift together first 3 ingredients. Combine remaining ingredients. Lightly grease a large, shallow pan. Spread mixture ½" thick. Bake in a 300° oven for 1 hour. Cut into squares and cool thoroughly. Grind in food chopper using coarse blade. Place in shallow pan and toast. Leave until dry and cool. Store in air-tight container. Serve with milk or yogurt.

Granola

1 c oil
1 c water
2 c honey

6 c rolled oats
6 c rolled wheat
1 c wheat germ

1 c roasted peanuts
1 c roasted chopped
   filberts (nuts can
   be substituted)
1 c roasted sunflower
   seeds
1 c wheat flour
1 c powdered milk

Mix oil, water and honey. In a large container, mix remaining ingredients. Pour honey mixture over and mix well. Spread on cookie sheets and toast in 250° oven 2 hours or until brown. Stir often to prevent burning. Cool in oven overnight to dry out. Add chopped dried fruit or raisins. Store in air-tight container. Serve with milk.

Wheat pancakes

2¼ c wheat mix (pg 100)
1½ cups water
1 beaten egg

Oat pancakes

1½ c oat mix (pg 101)
1 c water
1 beaten egg

Cornmeal pancakes

2 c cornmeal mix (pg 101)
2 c water
1 beaten egg

White pancakes

2 c white mix (pg 100)
1½ c water
2 beaten eggs

Beat egg and water. Add to mix and stir until moistened. Spoon onto hot greased griddle and cook until bubbles appear and become dry. Turn and cook until golden brown.

Serve with: Hot homemade syrup (pg 108)
               Peanut butter and applesauce
               Fruit
               Jams and jellies
               Spicy tomato sauce and cheese (pg 125)

Company Waffles

3 eggs, separated
½ c cooking oil
2 c buttermilk or milk
   with 2 Tbs vinegar added
2 c whole wheat flour

2 tsp baking powder
1 tsp baking soda
1 tsp salt

Mix ingredients (except egg whites) just until smooth. Beat egg whites until stiff. Gently fold into batter. Bake in greased waffle iron. Makes about 10   4″ square waffles.

Homemade Maple Syrup

2 c sugar
1 c water

¼ c karo syrup
1 tsp mapleine flavoring

Combine ingredients. Bring to a boil, stirring constantly to dissolve sugar. Cook 3 minutes.

Peach Pizza

Make pizza crust (pg 101)
Top with sliced peaches arranged attractively. Mix together:

1 Tbs margarine
½ c white mix (pg 100)
   or ½ c raw oats
½ c brown sugar

1 tsp cinnamon
¼ tsp nutmeg

Sprinkle sugar mixture over top of peaches. Bake at 450° for 15 minutes.

Wheat Crumb Cake

2 c wheat mix (pg 100)
1 c brown sugar
½ tsp cinnamon
¼ tsp nutmeg

½ c water
1 egg
½ c raisins
½ c chopped nuts (opt)

Combine wheat mix & sugar. Set aside ¼ c of mixture. To remaining mixture add cinnamon, nutmeg, water, eggs and raisins. Mix just until moistened. Pour into greased round cake pan. Sprinkle reserved mixture and nuts over top. Bake 350° for 30 minutes.

Get the Day Started Drink

1 c milk
1 c yogurt
1 c fruit

2 Tbs sugar or sweeten
   to taste
1 Tbs wheat germ
1 Tbs powdered brewers
   yeast

Blend together. If you use evaporated milk, blend several ice cubes.

21 BREAD SPREADS

Danish Openface Sandwiches

The Danes eat a great variety of delicious toppings on a very thin pressed rye bread. The sandwich is always eaten continental style. With the fork in the left hand and the knife in the right, the knife cuts and loads the food. Keep the fork in the left hand and lift the fork to your mouth. Do not transfer the utensils. Our kids think eating with continental manners is great fun and will try many foods they normally wouldn't enjoy!

Let's consider 2 openface toppings: vegetable and fruit.

Vegetable Toppings

Combine a can of drained vegetables with sour cream, yoga cheese, or homemade mayonnaise. Our favorites are peas, peas and carrots, beets and asparagus. Serve on a thin slice of whole wheat bread.

Fruit Toppings

Combine a can or bottle of drained, sliced fruit with sweetened yoga cheese or honey mayonnaise. We like fruit cocktail, peaches, apples. Serve on thinly sliced wheat or white bread.

Mayonnaise

1 egg
½ tsp dry mustard
¾ tsp salt

1½ Tbs cider vinegar
1 c salad oil

Using the blender on medium speed, blend egg with mustard and salt. Slowly add vinegar and oil while still blending. Stop blending when last of oil has been added. Makes about 1¼ cups.

Honey Mayonnaise (for fruit)

½ c mayonnaise
1 Tbs honey

1 Tbs lemon juice or
   equivalent extract
2 Tbs yoga cheese

Combine with chilled mayonnaise. Store tightly covered in refrigerator. Makes 1¼ cups.

Soybean Spread

1 c soybeans (cooked and
   pureed or use pulp
   from soy milk)
2 Tbs mayonnaise
1 Tbs pickle relish

½ tsp onion powder
pinch of salt

Mix together. Chill for 3 or more hours. Spread on bread. Serves 4.

Lentil Spread

1 lb cooked, mashed lentils
1 tsp onion powder
½ c oil or margarine

½ tsp garlic powder
1 Tbs marjoram
salt to taste

Combine and cook for 5 minutes. Cool. Put in tightly covered jar and refrigerate.

Soybean Extender

Place 1 c washed soybeans in nylon net bag in 5 to 6 cups water. Pressure cook for 30 minutes at 15 pounds. Puree in blender using 1 c liquid, or put through food chopper. Using half pureed soybeans, add to other sandwich foods such as peanut butter, tuna fish, avocado. The flavor of soy is mild and will absorb the other flavoring.

Toast and Fruit

Try wheat toast with honey, cinnamon and sliced fruit. You're back to basics!

22   SOUPS

What tastes more wholesome on cold winter days than a bowl of warm hearty soup and fresh homemade bread? The three basic soups that follow can be varied by adding vegetables, pasta products and seasonings. Experiment to see what you like.

Clear Soups

Make a broth using ham, beef or chicken soup base or bouillon. Add any combination of fresh, dried, canned or frozen vegetables, pasta products, tofu cubes or sprouts. Simmer 15 minutes or until the vegetables are done.

Cream Soups

Heat vegetable water and milk. Add beef, ham or chicken soup base or bouillon. Thicken with flour and water (a whisk makes this step a snap). Add cooked and pureed vegetables.

Bean and Pea Soups

Sort and wash beans. Soak overnight (use 4 times as much water as beans), or boil them for 5 minutes and let stand one hour in the hot water. Cook with salt, bouillon or soup base flavoring, about 3 hours or until beans are soft. The last hour, onion, carrot, celery, pepper flakes and seasonings may be added. Substitute canned tomatoes as part of the liquid for tasty flavor.

Family Favorites

Chicken Noodle and Vegetable Soup

(I can serve all the kids in my neighborhood for just pennies.)

1½ quarts boiling water
4 Tbs chicken soup base
or bouillon

1 c broken spaghetti
pieces
¼ c dried carrot flakes
½ c dried celery leaves

Simmer 15 minutes. Serve

Creamed Potato Soup

1 large peeled & cubed potato
or dried equivalent
5 c hot water
2 Tbs beef soup base or
bouillon cubes
2 c milk
1 c canned milk
3 Tbs flour

1 Tbs dried onion flakes,
crushed
⅛ tsp paprika
⅛ tsp Worchestershire
sauce
1 tsp salt (opt)
1 Tbs parsley flakes
1c yoga cheese (opt)
2 Tbs margarine

Combine first 3 ingredients. Cook until soft and mash. Add milk and canned milk. Make a paste of flour and water. Stir into hot potato mixture using a whisk. Stir constantly until soup is thick and smooth. Add remaining ingredients. Heat through. Serve in soup bowls with a pat of margarine on top.

Wheat Chili

3 c water
3 Tbs beef soup base
or bouillon
1½ c whole wheat
1 chopped onion or
dried equivalent
½ can tomatoes
½ can tomato soup
1 can tomato sauce

dash garlic
1 tsp chili powder
½ Tbs brown sugar
1 bay leaf
½ tsp sweet basil
½ tsp ground cumin

Simmer first 3 ingredients for 1 hour. Add remaining ingredients. Simmer 1 additional hour. Serves 6.

Lentil Soup

2 quarts water
2 c lentils washed
   in cold water
½ c dried celery leaves
¼ c each of dried
   carrots, onions, potatoes
1 tsp dried parsley

salt and pepper to taste
dash nutmeg
4 Tbs ham soup base
   or bouillon

Mix all ingredients. Cook slowly 1½ hours. Whisk ½ c flour in 1 c cold water. Thicken hot soup by adding flour mixture while stirring constantly. Serve in soup bowls with a pat of margarine on top.

Split Pea Soup

3 c whole or split peas
2½ quarts water
¼ c dried onion
½ c dried celery leaves

½ c dried diced carrots
5 Tbs ham flavored soup
   base or bouillon
½ tsp pepper
¼ tsp marjoram

Soak dried peas overnight or boil 5 minutes and let soak 1 hour. Combine all ingredients. Cook slowly for 2½ hours or until peas are soft. Serve as is or puree until smooth.

California Bean Soup

2 c white beans (rinsed)
2½ quarts water
1 quart tomatoes

¼ c dried onion
¼ c dried diced carrots
½ c chopped dried celery
   leaves
5-7 Tbs ham soup base
   or bouillon

Soak beans in water overnight or boil 5 minutes and soak 1 hour. Add 1 quart tomatoes. Cook 2 hours. Add remaining ingredients and cook until beans are soft, about 1 hour. Serve with hot homemade bread.

117

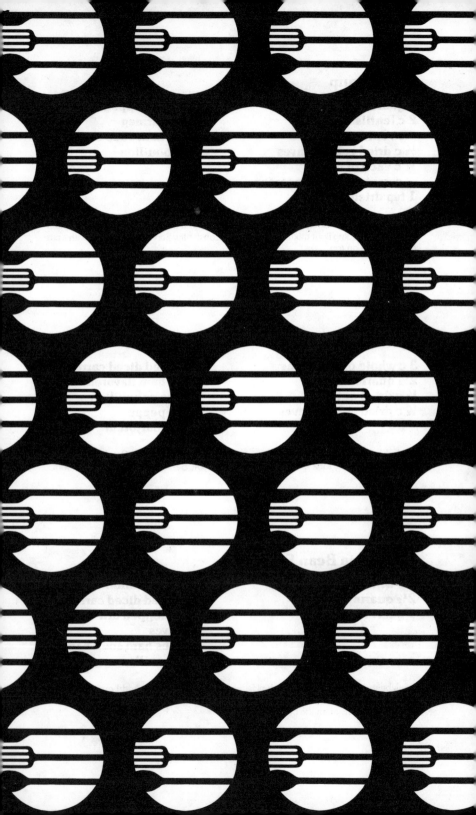

23 MAIN DISHES

Let's start with a good old American eating tradition - the hamburger (or a great substitute)!

Soy Sizzler Burgers

½ c dry soybeans
1 c raw rolled oats
½ c chopped nuts
1 medium onion or
  dry equivalent
1 Tbs oil

1 egg
½ c chopped celery
  or dry
  equivalent
½ tsp cumin
2 Tbs beef soup base
  or bouillon

Soak soybeans in 2 c water overnight. Drain water saving 1 c. Put beans in blender with 1 c water and egg. Blend until texture is fine. Add oats and nuts. Let stand 10 minutes. Add remaining ingredients. Mix well. Drop by tablespoonsful onto greased skillet. Fry at medium heat until brown on both sides and well done. Serve as a hamburger with all the trimmings, or as patties topped with gravy, hot tomato sauce or tarter sauce. They freeze well. Makes 21 patties.

Lentilburgers

1½ c dried lentils
6 c water
1 onion or
   dry equivalent

2 bay leaves
1 carrot, cut in pieces
   or dried equivalent
2 tsp salt

Wash lentils in cold water. Place all ingredients in a large saucepan. Bring to a boil, reduce heat and simmer, covered for 45 minutes. Drain and reserve ½ c cooking liquid. Discard onion and bay leaves. Place lentils, reserved ½ c cooking liquid, and carrot in blender and process until very smooth. Result: pureed lentils.

To make burger:

Pureed lentils
1 med onion, chopped
   or dry equivalent
¼ tsp garlic powder
1 rib celery or
   dried equivalent
3 Tbs chopped parsley

2 eggs
½ c each of cornmeal
   and wheat germ
6 Tbs molasses
2 Tbs vinegar
1½ tsp dry mustard

Mix all ingredients. To fry, spoon ¼ c mixture onto lightly greased skillet for each burger. Brown on both sides. To bake, spoon ¼ c of mixture for each burger onto greased foil-lined baking sheet. Bake 350° for 20 minutes. Serve hot.

Tuna Patties

1 can tuna fish
¼ c natural flavored TVP
   or soybeans which are
   soaked, cooked and pureed
½ c bread or cracker crumbs
½ tsp sweet basil

½ tsp salt
¼ tsp each pepper &
   thyme
2 tsp dried parsley
2 eggs, well beaten

Mix, form into patties. Fry in margarine or oil until golden brown.

Making a Complete Protein Roast or Casserole

Making a complete protein meal is a creative experience, if you follow the charts below. The Basic Roast is taken from *Recipes for Heart Disease-Preventive Cookery.*

Basic Roast Chart

Choose 1 from each of the following categories

Protein (2 cups)

kidney beans
lentils
garbanzos
tofu
cottage cheese
soy beans
etc.

Binding

3 Tbs potato flour
2 Tbs soy flour
½ c cooked oatmeal
½ c Cream of Wheat
3 Tbs tapioca
1 egg or 2 egg whites
3 Tbs wheat flour

Salt (1 tsp and/or)

chicken, ham, beef
   soup base or
   bouillon
soy sauce
garlic salt
onion salt
celery salt
etc.

Carbohydrate (1 c)

dried whole wheat
   bread crumbs
uncooked oatmeal
cooked brown rice
wheat germ
etc.

Liquid (1-1½ c as needed)

tomato sauce
broth from
   cooked or canned
   vegetables
milk or soy milk

Vegetable oil or Margarine (2 Tbs)

Onion or Dried Onion Flakes
(1 chopped or equivalent)

Nuts (½ c) chopped or ground

peanuts
cashews
almonds
walnuts
sunflower seeds
etc.

Seasoning (¼ tsp of one or more)

sage
cumin
oregano
thyme
rosemary
Italian seasoning
parsley
etc.

Casserole Chart

Choose one from each of the first 4 columns, topping with column 5. Add salt, pepper and seasonings of your choice. Seasonings are very important so experiment to find combinations you enjoy. Begin with suggestions from the chart on previous page.

1	2	3	4	5
2 c cooked	**1 c cooked**	**1½ c**	**1½ c cooked**	**3 to 5 Tbs**
whole wheat cereal	lima beans	cream sauce	celery & onions	wheat germ
brown rice	soy beans	tomatoes & cream sauce	mushrooms & bamboo shoots	slivered almonds
corn or corn meal	black beans or kidney beans	cottage cheese	green beans	brewer's yeast
millet	peas (can be raw)	mushrooms & cream sauce	carrots	whole wheat bread crumbs
whole wheat spaghetti	garbanzo beans	yogurt	onion & pimento	sunflower seeds
whole wheat noodles	peanuts	grated cheddar cheese or powder cheese	green pepper & onions	sesame seeds

Cooking With Sauces

Choose one sauce	Add one or more	Serve over
Basic white sauce	Boiled chopped eggs	Toast
Cheese sauce	Drained canned vegetables	Rice
Soup sauce	Drained tuna fish	Macaroni
Curry sauce	Chopped canned meat	Spaghetti
Sweet and Sour sauce	Gluten strips	Any noodles
Barbeque Sauce	Gluten sausage balls	Cooked potatoes
Spicy tomato sauce	Cooked beans or legumes	Sprouts
Beef Gravy	Cubed tofu	
Ham Gravy		
Chicken Gravy		

Top with 1 or more

Toasted sunflower or sesame
   seeds
Roasted nuts
Cottage cheese
Yoga cheese
Parmesan cheese
Shredded cheese
TVP seasoned bits such as
   baco bits
Shredded coconut
Chopped dry fruits
Raisins

Basic White Sauce

2 Tbs margarine or oil
¼ c chopped onion or
   dry equivalent (opt)
¼ c flour

2 c milk
½ tsp salt
⅛ tsp pepper
Additional seasonings

Melt the margarine. If you want to add onions, saute them until soft. Remove from heat, mix in flour, salt and pepper. Return to heat slowly adding milk, stirring constantly with whisk. When smooth, continue cooking and stir with spoon until thick. Season with garlic powder, worchestershire sauce, paprika, etc. for a different flavor.

Cheese Sauce

¾ c powdered cheese (approx)
2 c water or milk

⅛ tsp pepper

Beat powdered cheese into water. Add pepper and cook, stirring constantly until thick.
   OR
Make basic white sauce and add 1 c grated cheese. Cook until cheese is melted. Salt to taste.

Soup Sauce

Heat a can of undiluted cream soup (mushroom, celery, chicken). Add ¼ c milk.
    OR
Add can of undiluted cream soup to basic white sauce.

Curry Sauce

½ c margarine
1 large minced onion
    or dry equivalent
½ c flour
1 Tbs curry powder
    (vary according to
    taste)

2 Tbs chicken soup base
    or bouillon
1½ c hot water
1 can evaporated milk
    or 1½ c milk

Saute onion in margarine. Remove from heat, add flour, curry powder, chicken flavoring and hot water. Mix well. Return to heat, stirring constantly til thick. Add milk. (Curry Sauce is very good with 8 boiled, quartered eggs, served over rice and topped with roasted peanuts, raisins, coconut and relish.)

Sweet and Sour Sauce

1 c sugar
½ c vinegar
¾ c water
1 tsp dried green pepper
    flakes

½ tsp salt
1 tsp corn starch
1 Tbs cold water
1 tsp paprika

Mix first 5 ingredients in saucepan. Simmer 5 minutes. Combine corn starch and cold water. Add slowly to hot mixture while stirring constantly. Cook until thick. Add paprika. (Try adding sausage gluten balls and top with slivered almonds. Serve over rice.)

Barbeque Sauce

2 medium onions,
    chopped (or dry
    equivalent)
½ c chopped celery or
¼ c dried chopped
    celery leaves
1 c catsup
1¼ c water

¼ c vinegar
3 Tbs worchestershire
    sauce
2 Tbs each brown sugar,
    prepared mustard
Salt and pepper to taste

Saute onion and celery in margarine. Add all ingredients. Simmer 15 minutes.

Spicy Tomato Sauce

2 cans tomato sauce
1 Tbs sweet basil
¼ tsp garlic powder

1½ tsp chili powder
⅛ tsp cayenne pepper
**1 Tbs dried onion flakes,
  crushed**

Combine ingredients. Simmer 15 minutes.

Beef, Ham, Chicken Gravy

Make basic white sauce and add 1 Tbs beef, ham or chicken soup base for each cup sauce. Cook and stir until dissolved.

OR

Mix ¼ cup flour into 1 cup cold water. Add 1 cup hot water and 2 Tbs beef, ham or chicken soup base. Bring to boil, stirring constantly until thick. ⅛ tsp each of thyme and sage taste great added to chicken gravy.

Family Favorites
Stewed Tomato Casserole

**6 slices cubed
  whole wheat bread**
**¼ c each onion, celery,
  green pepper flakes**
**1 quart chopped tomatoes
  (juice and all)**
1 8 oz. can tomato sauce

1 tsp salt
¼ tsp pepper
**½ tsp worchestershire
  sauce**
grated cheese (opt)

Put bread into oiled casserole dish. Combine all other ingredients and pour over bread. Bake at 350° for 20 minutes. Before baking sprinkle grated cheese on top for added nutrition and taste.

Spaghetti Sauce

2 cans tomato sauce
1¾ c water
1 Tbs beef soup base
1 Tbs green pepper flakes
1 Tbs onion flakes
¼ tsp oregano
¼ tsp garlic powder

⅛ tsp sage
⅛ tsp thyme
1 tsp basil
1 Tbs chopped parsley
1 sm bay leaf
½ tsp sugar

Combine ingredients in a saucepan. Slowly cook for ½ hour. Serve over noodles topped with grated parmesan or romano cheese.

Refried Beans

1 lb. dried pinto or
   pink beans, rinsed
5½ c water
½ c dried onions

½ c margarine,
   or shortening
salt to taste

Soak beans in water overnight or boil 5 minutes and let sit 1 hour. Add onions. Bring to a boil and simmer slowly about 3 hours or until beans are very tender. Mash beans with potato masher. Add margarine & salt. Mix well and continue cooking, stirring frequently until beans are thick and margarine is absorbed.

Tostados

Place a large tortilla (pg 99) flat on plate. Top with refried beans (pg 126) or lentil spread (pg 112), spicy tomato sauce (pg 125), reconstituted powdered cheese, lots of sprouts (pg 61), and top with seasoned yoga cheese (pg 69). Be creative. Add what you like!

Cheese Pie

Crust

2 c flour
1 tsp salt
1 tsp sugar

⅔ c oil
3 Tbs milk

Sift first 3 ingredients together and put into pie pan. Using a fork, whip milk into oil until foamy. Make a well in flour, pour in oil mixture and stir only until flour is moist. Using hands, pat dough into 2   9″ pie pans.

Filling

1 can drained vegetables
3 c milk
¾ c powdered cheese
5 well beaten eggs
¼ tsp sweet basil

⅛ tsp pepper
dash cayenne pepper
½ tsp worchestershire
  sauce
1 tsp onion powder

Arrange drained vegetables on bottom of both pie crusts. Using part of milk, whisk powdered cheese until smooth. Add to milk. Add all other ingredients. Pour equally into both crusts. Bake 350° for 1 hour.

Macaroni, Cheese and Tuna

2 c dry macaroni
2 quarts boiling water
1 tsp salt
½ cube margarine
¾ c powdered cheese
½ c milk

1 tsp worchestershire
  sauce
⅛ tsp pepper
1 tsp prepared mustard
1 can drained tuna
1 quart chopped
  tomatoes
  or 1 can tomato sauce

Boil macaroni in salted water for 15 minutes. Drain. Add margarine. In separate bowl, whisk powdered cheese into milk until smooth. Add worchestershire sauce, pepper and mustard. Pour over macaroni and mix well. Add flaked tuna and chopped tomatoes. Stir over heat for 2 to 3 minutes. Serve.

Main Dishes
Sausage Gluten Balls or Patties

2 c ground gluten
2 beaten eggs
2 Tbs oil
½ tsp dried onion flakes
  crushed
2 Tbs flour

Sausage flavoring
  1¼ tsp salt
  2 tsp sage
  1 tsp black pepper
  ¼ tsp cloves
  ½ tsp nutmeg
  ½ tsp sugar

Combine spices. Combine all ingredients and form walnut sized balls or flat patties. Place on cookie sheet and bake 20 minutes at 350° to firm them up. Fry in a little oil until heated through.

Gluten Parmesan

2 Tbs margarine or oil
4 beef steaklets
⅔ c canned milk

½ c plus 2 Tbs parmesan
   cheese
½ c flour
1   8 oz can tomato sauce

Melt margarine in an 8″ × 12″ pan in a 350° oven. Dip steaklets in ⅓ cup milk, then in mixture of 2 Tbs parmesan cheese and flour. Put in pan and bake 30 minutes. Mix remaining milk and cheese. Pour tomato sauce around steaklets. Spoon cheese mix on steaklets. Bake 350° for 20 to 25 minutes. Serves 4.

Larsen's Roni Rice

¼ c margarine or oil
1 c rice
½ c broken spaghetti
   (about 1″ pieces)

2½ c hot water
1 tsp turmeric
2 Tbs chicken soup base
   or bouillon

Saute rice and spaghetti in margarine until browned, stirring constantly. Add hot water & spices. Stir. Cover and simmer for ½ hour or until moisture is absorbed.

FAVORITE RECIPES

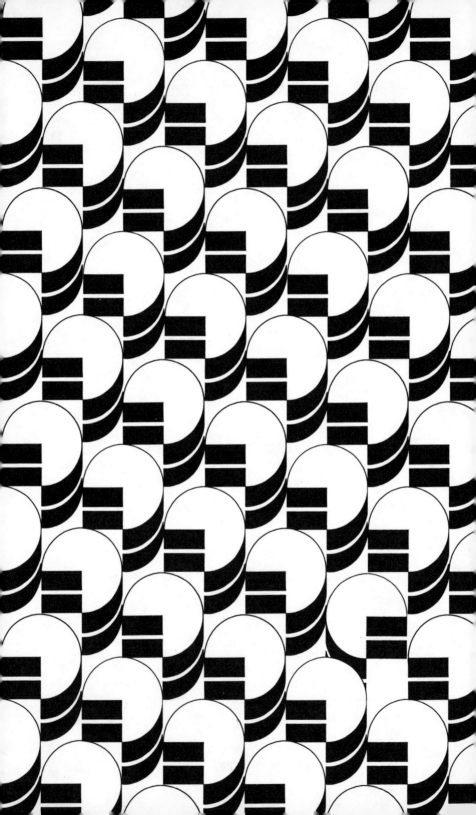

24 SNACKS & DESSERTS

Fine Salt

Blend 1 cup iodized salt in blender until very fine (about 3 minutes). Keep in air-tight container. Use sparingly for roasted nuts and popcorn.

Roasted Nuts

1 lb nuts	**OR**	**1 lb nuts**
2 Tbs worchestershire		**2 tsp oil**
sauce		**1 tsp fine salt**
1 tsp fine salt		
(see above)		

Stir until nuts are thoroughly coated. Spread evenly on cookie sheet. Bake 250° degrees for 1 hour stirring every 15 minutes.

Roasted soybeans

1 c dry soybeans	**1 tsp fine salt**
3 c water	**¼ tsp onion or garlic**
2 tsp oil or soy sauce	**powder if desired**

Wash soybeans and soak overnight in refrigerator. Add salt and bring to a boil. Simmer 1 hour. (To prevent boiling over add ½ tsp oil.) Remove from heat. Drain well. Stir with oil or soy sauce until salt & seasonings are well coated. Spread in shallow pan. Bake, stirring frequently at 250° for 1 hour or until lightly browned.

Campers Mix

3 c Spanish or Virginia
  peanuts
3 c sunflower seeds
1 c broken cashews

3 c raisins or chopped
  dates
2 c carob chips

In separate pans, spread peanuts and sunflower seeds. Roast at 250° for 1 hour, stirring frequently. Remove from oven when golden. Cool. Add other ingredients and mix well. Be creative with this recipe. Add any combination of nuts and dry fruit. Store in air-tight containers.

Fruit Nut Balls

1 c dried fruit
  (firmly packed)
1 c roasted nuts

2 tsp peanut butter
¼ c honey

Using the small disc on the meat grinder, grind dry fruit and nuts together. Mix remaining ingredients and shape into balls. If you like, roll balls in toasted sesame seeds. Experiment to see what combinations you enjoy.

Peanut Butter Candy

Combine equal portions of: peanut butter
    honey
    powdered milk

Knead well. Roll into a rope and cut into 1″ pieces. Roll each piece in roasted sesame seeds, chopped coconut, coat with dipping chocolate, or wrap individually. Store in refrigerator.

Honey Taffy

2 c honey

Cook in heavy saucepan to hard crack stage (285° F). Pour onto buttered platter. With a spatula fold cooled edges into the center until candy is very warm but can be handled. Pull it with fingers until honey is light colored, slightly stringy and looses its gloss. Roll into a rope and cut with scissors. Wrap individually. Taffy making is a great family activity!

Sesame Seed Candy

1 c sesame seeds
¼ c margarine
½ c light corn syrup

1 c sugar
½ tsp vanilla
¼ tsp salt

Toast sesame seeds 10 minutes at 350°. Melt margarine. Add corn syrup and sugar. Cook over high heat stirring frequently until 290°. Remove from heat, add sesame seeds, vanilla and salt and pour immediately onto buttered baking sheet. Let stand until cool then break into pieces.

3 Minute, Never Fail, Creamy Fudge

¼ lb margarine, melted
¼ c canned milk
½ c cocoa powder

pinch salt
1 lb pkg powdered sugar
½ c chopped nuts (opt)

Mix all together. Add chopped nuts. Spread into a buttered pan. Chill and cut.

5 Minute, Never Fail, Creamy Penuche

½ c margarine, melted
1 c brown sugar

½ c canned milk
1¾ to 2 c powdered sugar
1 c chopped nuts (opt)

Cook margarine and brown sugar over low heat for 2 minutes stirring constantly. Add milk and continue cooking and stirring until mixture boils. Remove from heat. Cool. Gradually add powdered sugar until fudge consistently is reached. Add nuts. Spread in a buttered 8″ square pan. Chill and cut.

Carmel Corn

This is the only time I buy gourmet popcorn instead of using my pigeon popcorn. I don't want one kernal!

1 c margarine
2 c brown sugar
½ c corn syrup

1 tsp salt
½ tsp baking soda
1 tsp vanilla
6 quarts popped popcorn

Melt butter. Stir in next 3 ingredients. Bring to a boil, stirring constantly. Boil without stirring, for 5 minutes. Remove from heat, stir in baking soda and vanilla. Gradually pour over popcorn. Mix well. Turn into 2 large shallow baking pans. Bake in 250° F oven 1 hour stirring every 15 minutes. Remove from oven. When completely cool, separate and store in tightly covered container.

Seasoned Popcorn

Sprinkle popped corn with garlic salt, onion salt, chili powder or powdered cheese.

Corn chips

These are delicious dipped in homemade mayonnaise!

3 c drained chopped
   canned tomatoes
¼ c chopped onion or
   dried equivalent
4 c finely ground dried
   sweet corn or field corn

2 Tbs oil
1 tsp each cayenne, dried
   dill weed and salt
⅛ tsp garlic powder

Mix ingredients and spread as thin as possible on parchment paper. When it seems quite dry, remove the paper and dry on screen until very crisp.

Corn Nuts

Dry your own on the cob by hanging it by the husk in a dry warm area. When completely dry, remove the whole kernals from cob. Place some kernals in a pan and shake constantly over high heat. Add margarine, fine salt and seasonings.

Popped Wheat

Shake the whole kernal wheat in a pan over high heat until popped. Add fine salt and seasoning.

Tortilla Chips

Make tortillas (pg 99).
Cut tortillas into pie shaped wedges. Fry a few at a time in 1" of hot oil until they are crisp and lightly browned (1 minute or less). Drain on paper towels and sprinkle with fine salt and seasonings.

Graham Crackers

½ c evaporated milk
  (or ⅓ c dry milk
  powder plus ½ c water)
2 Tbs vinegar
1 c brown sugar
½ c white sugar
1 c oil

6c whole wheat or
  graham flour
1 tsp salt
1 tsp soda
1½ tsp vanilla
2 beaten eggs

Mix milk and vinegar. In another bowl blend sugars, oil, vanilla and eggs. Combine. Add flour, salt and soda. Mix well. Divide mixture in four equal parts. Place each on greased and floured cookie sheet. Roll from center to edges until about ⅛" thick. Prick with a fork. Bake at 375° for 15 minutes or until light brown. Remove from oven and cut into squares immediately. Makes 60.

Country Crisp Crackers

1 c corn meal
1½ c whole wheat flour
2 Tbs brown sugar
½ tsp salt

½ c margarine
1 to 2 Tbs crushed dry
  onion flakes
½ c water

Mix well. Place on greased cookie sheet. Beginning from the center, roll ⅛" thick. Cut into squares and prick with a fork. Sprinkle salt and bake at 350° for 15 minutes.

Soft Brown Sugar Cookies

1½ c margarine
2 c brown sugar
1 beaten egg
4 c flour

Cream sugar and margarine. Add beaten egg and flour. Mix well. Chill 2 hours. Roll ⅛" thick and cut into shapes. Bake at 350° for 8-10 minutes. For giant cookies, roll dough ¼" thick on cookie sheet. Cut out cookie and bake at 350° for 12 minutes. Cool on cookie sheet.

Danish Fruit with Cream

Puree any fruit or fruit combination or use fruit juice. (We like strawberries & rhubarb [strained], plums, raspberries, apple cider.) Sweeten to taste. To 1 quart juice add 2 Tbs corn starch. Cook over medium heat, stirring constantly until thick. Serve hot or cold with canned milk or whipped topping.

Oat Crumb Cake

2 c oat mix (pg 101)
1 c brown sugar
¼ tsp cinnamon

¼ tsp nutmeg
½ c water
1 egg

Combine mix and sugar. Set aside ¼ c of mixture. To remaining mixture, add spices, water, egg and stir until thoroughly blended. Spread dough in greased 8″ square pan and sprinkle with reserved crumbs. Bake at 350° for 30 minutes.

Cherry Rice Dessert

1 quart milk
1¾ c rice
1 tsp salt

Whipped topping (pg 140)
½ c slivered almonds
   or filberts
Cherry glaze topping

Combine milk, rice and salt in heavy saucepan with tight fitting lid. Bring to boil. Turn heat down and simmer 40 minutes or until milk is absorbed. Cool, then refrigerate. When chilled, fold in nuts and whipped topping. Serve with cherry glaze topping.

Cherry Glaze Topping

1 quart pitted pie
   cherries
Sugar to taste

2 Tbs corn starch
red food coloring (opt)

Drain cherry juice. Add water to make 2 cups. Add sugar and corn starch. Cook, stirring constantly until thick and clear. Add cherries and red food coloring. Serve warm over cold rice.
    Cherry Rice dessert is a Christmas tradition with our family. Rice is served in a large bowl. One whole nut is hidden in the rice. As the bowl is passed around the table, each person serves himself. Cherry topping is served, everyone eats very carefully because the person finding the whole nut receives a little gift.

Rice Pudding

2 c cold boiled rice
3 c hot milk
¼ c molasses
¼ c raisins

1 Tbs margarine
¾ tsp salt
½ tsp nutmeg

Mix rice and hot milk. Add remaining ingredients. Pour into a buttered baking dish and bake at 350° for 1 hour. Stir once or twice during the first ½ hour.

Vanilla Pudding

⅓ c sugar
3 Tbs cornstarch
¼ tsp salt

2½ c canned milk
(or use part milk)
1½ tsp vanilla

Mix dry ingredients. Blend in milk. Heat, stirring constantly until mixture thickens. Cook 2 to 3 minutes more. Add vanilla. Pour into serving dishes and chill. Serves 4.

Chocolate Pudding

Follow recipe for vanilla pudding but increase sugar to ½ cup and mix ⅓ cup cocoa with sugar and cornstarch. Serve with canned milk.

Caramel Pudding

Melt ½ cup sugar in heavy pan over low heat, stirring until medium brown. Remove from heat. Slowly add ½ cup boiling water. Return to heat and stir until lumps dissolve. Combine ¼ cup sugar, 3 Tbs cornstarch, and ¼ tsp salt in saucepan. Blend in 2 cups milk. Stir in caramel syrup. Cook over medium heat stirring constantly until thick. Cook 2 minutes more. Add 1½ tsp vanilla. Pour into 5 rinsed molds. Chill.

Applesauce Dessert

1 c whole wheat
   bread crumbs or
   crushed graham crackers
¼ c melted margarine
2 Tbs sugar

Applesauce
Whipped canned milk or
   whipped topping
   (pg 140)

In fry pan toast bread crumbs or graham crackers in melted margarine. Sprinkle sugar over while stirring with a spoon. When crispy, remove from heat and put in dessert dishes. Cover with applesauce and top with whipped canned milk or whipped topping. Serve immediately.

Whipped Canned Milk

In deep bowl, chill canned milk in freezer until crystals form around edge. Slowly add ¼ cup sugar while beating with chilled beaters. Whip until stiff. Serve immediately.

Frozen Yogurt

Once you're accustomed to homemade frozen yogurt, you won't settle for less. The fresh, sweet flavor just can't be replaced by other frozen desserts. Once you have made yogurt, add any combination of fruit and sweetener you enjoy. Some favorites:

Fancy Frozen Yogurt

4 c fruit	**¼ tsp each salt and**
1 c sugar	**cream of tartar**
4 tsp vanilla	**¼ c sugar**
2 Tbs lemon juice	**2 quarts yogurt**
3 eggs, separated	

Combine fruit and sugar in pan. Bring to boil stirring constantly. Lower heat and cook 1 to 4 minutes stirring until fruit is softened. Stir in lemon juice and vanilla. Beat egg yolks. Using a whisk, whip yolks into fruit mixture. Cool to room temperature. Combine egg whites, salt and cream of tartar. Beat gradually adding sugar until stiff peaks are formed. Mix yogurt and fruit. Gently fold in egg whites. Freeze in a four quart ice cream freezer.

Frozen Orange Yogurt

1 gallon homemade yogurt
  (pg 67)
2 c sugar
1 12 oz can frozen orange concentrate

Freeze yogurt in a large covered bowl until ice crystals form around edge. Beat in blender adding 2 cups sugar and juice concentrate. Freeze again for several hours until slushy. Blend again until smooth and freeze. This texture has the consistency of soft ice cream when allowed to stand at room temperature 15 minutes before serving. If you want smoother texture, blend it more than twice, or freeze in ice cream freezer.

Frozen Strawberry Yogurt

1 gallon homemade yogurt
1 quart pureed strawberries
2 bananas
¼ c lemonade concentrate
2 c sugar

In a blender, combine all ingredients. Freeze. See discussion in frozen orange yogurt recipe.

Frozen Jello Yogurt

**One 3 oz pkg any
flavor jello
1 c sugar
½ c boiling water**

**2 quarts homemade
yogurt**

Dissolve jello and sugar in boiling water. Cool. Combine with yogurt. Freeze. See discussion in frozen orange yogurt recipe.

Sweetened Condensed Milk

**½ c hot water
1 c sugar**

**2 c instant dried milk
or 1½ c non instant
dried milk
⅛ c margarine**

Heat water and sugar until sugar is dissolved. Pour into a blender. Add margarine and milk, little at a time while blending until smooth. Refrigerate. This is the equivalent of 1-15 oz. can of commercial product.

Cherry Topped Cream Pie

Graham Cracker Crust

**1½ c crushed graham
crackers
½ c melted margarine**
Mix together and press into pie plate.

Filling

**1½ c sweetened
condensed milk (pg 139)
1 c thick yoga cheese (pg 69)**

**⅛ c bottled lemon juice
1 tsp vanilla**

Blend together. Pour into crust and refrigerate.

Topping:

**1 pint bottle pitted
pie cherries
2 Tbs corn starch**

**½ c sugar or to
desired taste
¼ tsp red food coloring
(opt)**

Drain juice. Add water to equal one cup. Add corn starch and sugar. Stirring constantly, bring to boil. Cook until thick and clear. Add food coloring. Cool. Add cherries. Pour over pie. Refrigerate at least 5 hours before serving.

Navy Bean Bundt Cake

This is a grand prize winning cake!

1⅔ c cooked navy
   beans
1 c margarine softened
1 c granulated sugar
⅔ c brown sugar,
   firmly packed
1 Tbs vanilla extract
2 eggs
2 c sifted flour

1½ tsp baking powder
1 tsp baking soda
2½ tsp nutmeg
2 tsp cinnamon
⅓ c evaporated milk
⅓ c water
½ c chopped pecans
1⅓ c flaked coconut

Puree beans in blender. Set aside. In large bowl, combine margarine, sugars and vanilla; beat until creamy. At high speed, add eggs, one at a time. Stir beans into sugar mixture. In medium bowl, combine flour, baking powder, baking soda, nutmeg and cinnamon. Alternately add dry ingredients with milk and water until blended. Add pecans and coconut; blend. Turn batter into greased and floured bundt pan. Bake in preheated, 350° oven for 50 to 55 minutes or until toothpick inserted comes out clean.

Fruit Cocktail Cake

1 beaten egg
1 tsp soda
¼ tsp salt
1 c sugar

1 - 1 lb can fruit
   cocktail (juice and all)
1 c flour
1 c brown sugar
1 c chopped nuts

Combine first 6 ingredients. Pour into 8" square pan. Top with brown sugar & nuts. Bake at 375° for 40-45 minutes or until center is firm. Serve with whipped topping.

Whipped Topping

1 tsp unflavored gelatin
2 tsp cold water
3 Tbs boiling water
½ c ice water

½ c nonfat dry milk
   powder
3 Tbs sugar
3 Tbs oil

Chill a small mixing bowl. In another bowl soften gelatin in 2 tsp cold water; add boiling water, stirring until gelatin is completely dissolved. Cool until tepid. Place ice water and milk powder in chilled mixing bowl and beat at high speed until mixture forms soft peaks. Gradually add sugar, while beating, then oil and gelatin mixture. Place in freezer for about 15 minutes, then transfer to refrigerator until ready to use. To restore a creamy texture, stir before serving. Makes 2 cups.

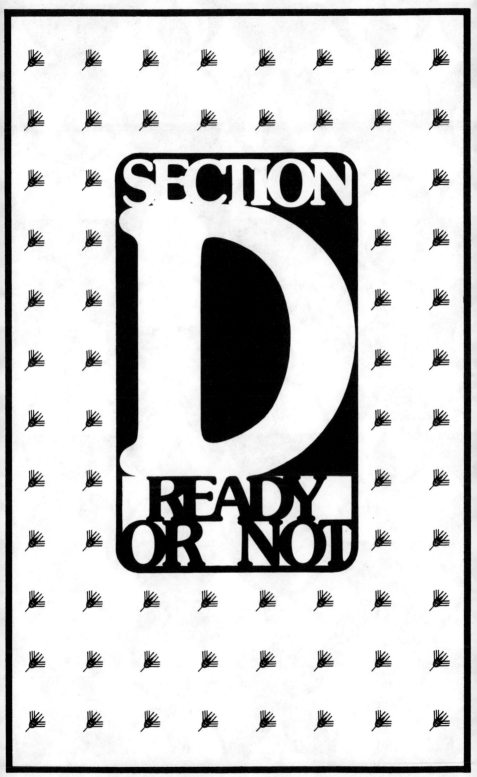

SECTION

D

READY
OR NOT

25 EMERGENCY COOKING

Natural disasters or extended power failures can be frightening and awesome if we are not prepared. When prepared, we meet emergencies with some confidence. If conventional cooking and heating methods are disrupted, there are alternatives — for instance:

COOKING METHODS

Wood or coal stoves offer the easiest way to cook and heat. One-pot meals and baking bread in a single pan could return us to easy, basic, but nourishing meals.

Some **kerosene portable heaters** are designed with a flat upper surface usable for cooking.

Camp stoves are easy to use for outdoor cooking. Fuels should be stored outdoors.

A charcoal barbeque grill, or a **wheel barrow lined with sand** can be used to burn charcoal or wood. *NEVER* burn charcoal indoors; it releases carbon monoxide and is dangerous.

A **fireplace** offers a variety of cooking possibilities. The best wood for cooking is hardwood like oak, hickory, black locust, hard maple or birch. When wood is not available, logs can be made from newspaper. Roll newspapers from corner to corner, tucking in the ends as you go, secure with a strip of wire. Even better logs can be made beforehand by soaking the logs in water and allowing them to dry. The Oregon State Extension Service recommends newspaper logs as a clean source of cooking heat.

A flat fireplace grate can be turned over and a fire built below. Use heavy cast iron kettles on this surface for cooking. Soap bottom and sides of pans before using for easier cleanup. If the grate is not usable, place a metal grill on bricks stacked on either side of the fireplace. Place your pans on the grill. A reflector oven (page 145) can be used in front of the fireplace. Take utmost care to prevent sparks from jumping onto carpets, etc. Close the fireplace screen everytime you leave the fire.

Wrap meats, vegetables, potatoes and other foods in heavy weight foil, place them directly in the hot coals and roast for **foil cooking.**

Pit cooking. Dig a pit, outside, approximately 9″ to 12″ deep and wide enough to comfortably hold a dutch oven. Line the bottom with dry material, like foil, sand, etc. Build your fire with wood or charcoal. When the wood has burned to a charcoal state, place your dutch oven on the coals. Pile coals on top of dutch oven or food will probably burn on bottom before the top is done. Some outdoor stores sell **heavy dutch ovens with legs.** Cook outdoors on concrete by building a charcoal fire on top of a piece of foil. Place dutch oven over hot coals, and shovel a few coals onto the lid of the oven to assure *even* heat. Lift the lid with a stick — it's hot!

You can **bake in a dutch oven** or a large pan with a tight fitting lid. Place a rack or metal lid on the bottom of the pan. Set your bread or cake on rack, allowing air to circulate around the sides and bottom. Cover with lid and place your pan or dutch oven on the heat source and bake.

A reflector oven operates by reflecting the heat of a blazing fire off a shiny surface. Make a reflector oven from a 5 gallon square can. Cut off one side (being careful not to damage the rest of the can). Wire each corner of the side panel to the center of the can, making a shelf. To bake, place reflector oven with open side facing flame. If you hold your hand in front of the flame and count to 5 before it becomes uncomfortable, the flame is about 350 degrees. Small items, such as cookies, biscuits, cupcakes bake most successfully.

A number 10 can stove. Near the open end of a #10 can cut a hole approximately 2″ × 4″ for adding fuel (the other end is the cooking surface). Use a can opener to make a number of holes around the top to let the smoke escape. Sticks, wood chips, charcoal, solid alcohol or a buddy burner provide fuel for a tin can stove. Be sure to stand stove on something solid that will not burn, like bricks, stone, or asbestos. Cook directly on the top or use the top as a burner for your pan. Make oven by placing another large empty can over the cooking area.

Buddy burners can be made from flat tuna or pineapple cans. Cut a strip of corrugated cardboard ¼″ higher than the can and coil it snuggly inside. Fill can with melted paraffin or candle wax. After the wax is hardened, light the paraffin and place inside Number 10 can stove or use as limited source of heat. Save the tuna can lid for extinguishing the burner.

26 FIRST AID EVACUATION KITS

Every day astounding things happen in medicine. Miracles happen because of increased knowledge of medical and related professions. We can increase our know-how to benefit us daily as well as during an emergency. The Red Cross offers classes on Home Nursing, CPR, and First Aid. The books *Standard First-aid and Personal Safety Handbook* (published by the Red Cross), and *Family Guide Emergency Health Care* (published by the U.S. Department of Defense and the U.S. Department of Health, Education and Welfare) offer a wide scope of information on care for the sick and injured.

First-aid and medical supplies should be on hand in our homes. Needs vary, depending on the ages and number of people in the family. (Remember to include and rotate specific medications or items used daily.) Keep in a sturdy container, well marked, and easily accessible to responsible adults. (List all items either inside or outside the container to facilitate immediate location and use.) Keep them out of the reach of smaller children, but make sure they know where the supplies are located.

HOME FIRST-AID KIT

scissors
tweezers
knife
razor blades
package of needles
safety pins
measuring cup
medicine dropper
oral & rectal
   thermometer
hot water bottle
   with syringe attach-
   ment for enema
ice bag
elastic bandages
sling material
triangular bandages
   (sheeting or soft
   fabric cut into a
   41" square diagonal)

6 rolls guaze bandages
adhesive tape
package of assorted
   bandages
wooden splints - 2 each
   ($\frac{1}{2}''\times3''\times14''$ &
   $\frac{1}{2}''\times4''\times30''$)
rope for rescue
wool blanket
flashlight & batteries
   (check regularly)
bar of soap
First-Aid Handbook

Ipecac Syrup (induces vomiting. Not to be used if strong
   corrosive or a petroleum product has been swallowed)
Powdered Activated Charcoal (to absorb swallowed
   poison)
Bicarbonate of Soda (baking soda)
Ammonia (small bottle of aromatic spirits to revive a
   person)
Calamine Lotion (for sunburn and insect bites)
Rubbing Alcohol (multipurpose)
Sterile Saline - Bring 1 pint water to a boil, add 1 tsp salt,
   cap in an air-tight bottle (Use for washing sores, eyes,
   etc.)
Diarrhea Preparation

Antibiotic Ointment
Aspirin and baby aspirin
A and D ointment or petroleum jelly

A smaller first-aid kit should be kept in the car. You might want an emergency kit including survival items, extra clothing, food and tools.

CAR FIRST-AID KIT (fits in a 3 lb. shortening can)

Petroleum jelly
A small package of absorbent cotton or cotton balls
Several packages of sterile gauze dressings 2" to 4" square
Assorted bandages ½" to 2" wide
Triangular bandage (sheeting or soft fabric made by cutting a 41" square diagonally)
A small pair of tweezers & scissors
A clinical thermometer
Safety pins, package of needles, sewing kit, rubber bands
Tongue blades or wooden applicator sticks
Aspirin
Prescribed medicines if needed (keep these up to date)
Insect repellent stick or Vitamin E tablets (when swallowed they produce a body odor that repels insects)
First-Aid Handbook (very important)

CAR EMERGENCY KIT   Can be packed in a suitcase.
Medical: Take car first-aid kit
Survival:
9' × 12' drop cloth for every 3 people (for a shelter)
100 feet of 200 lb test 100% nylon twine (to make a shelter, tools, furniture, etc.)
Aluminum space blanket for each person
Wool blankets (even when wet, wool retains 90% of heat)
Several large plastic garbage bags (for use as a ground cloth, to hold garbage, to make into raincoats, etc.)

6 five hour candles (for light, heat and to start fires)
Matches, waterproofed with nailpolish or paraffin, or in a
  waterproof container, and a Bic lighter
1 pkg of fine steel wool (to make fires, scour pans, etc.)
Compass with instructions (and knowledge to use it)
3 car flares - two each of 15, 30 and 45 minute flares (to
  start fires, give light, signal)
Paper and pencil (to leave messages)
Scout Field Book or Scout Merit Badge Book on Survival
  (very important for the inexperienced survivalist)

Food   (Enough for 3 days)
Plastic container of wheat
Canned protein (tuna, pork and beans, etc.) *and* a can
  opener
Peanut butter in plastic container
Crackers
Nuts, dried fruits, campers mixes
Freeze dried packages of vegetables, main dishes, soups
Powdered milk
Canteen, 2½ gallon collapsible water tote with spout
Water purification tablets
Collapsible cups, utensils, plates, tablecloth
6 piece scout aluminum mess kit and/or a large shortening
  can (to be used as kettle or container for food items)
Tin foil — cut into large squares (for foil cooking, making a
  fry pan, fire building when the ground is wet, etc.)
Washcloths and rags, bar of ivory soap or dishwashing
  soap

Clothes:
A complete change of clothes per person (wool if in a
  cold area)
A warm sweatshirt or sweater per person
Personal items (toilet paper in a plastic bag, shaving kit,
comb, etc.)

Tools:
Swiss pocket knife (one with screwdriver, can opener, etc.)
Tool kit with a collapsible shovel, saw and ax
Hammer, nails, pliers, screwdriver
A 5" file (to sharpen ax)

During natural disaster or war, all skills and preparation will be vital. An evacuation kit would be necessary, as well as useful. If you heard a flood or tornado were approaching and you had ½ hour to prepare to leave your house, what would you take? Suppose an earthquake occurred and within minutes an aftershock was expected which would probably destroy your home. What would you gather to take with you when you left? If you had an evacuation kit containing minimum basic survival items packed in a suitcase or in back packs, within minutes you could evacuate. This list was made by an experienced scouter who considered items that are light weight, multipurpose, and available in most outdoor stores. For your convenience and comfort you may want to include additional (what he calls "luxury") items.

Dreadful problems follow severe disaster. The lack of clean water supply is one *major* problem. Another is the spread of disease ultimately causing death. Doctors recommend immunizations be kept up to date, particularly tetanus, which requires a booster at least every 10 years.

EVACUATION KITS
Include minimum survival gear packed in backpacks or suitcases. Use the Car First-Aid and Emergency Kit suggestions and include the following:

Medical:
A snake bite kit

Survival:

Include a 2 man backpacking tent (can hold 3 children) for every 2 to 3 people (the 9' × 12' drop cloth can make a shelter but is not as comfortable as a tent)

A small crystal radio (no batteries are needed)

225 ft of 100 lb test fishing line and #12 and #2 fish hooks

Wire - 5 to 10 ft, light and flexible for snares to catch animals

Whistle (to tell others where you are)

Duct tape or adhesive tape - 1" by at least 12" (to repair various things)

Heavy duty surgical mask for each person

Old unfolded-type diapers - 2 per person (to use as bandannas, slings, rags, diapers, etc.)

Clothespins

Newspaper (to start fires or to crumple between clothing for added warmth)

Diapers, etc. if applicable

Food:

Plan lightweight, nutritious foods for 2 weeks (enough to get by, not to feast!)

A back packing propane stove with a cylinder or propane or a battery operated portable stove

Increase the 5 hour candles to 15 candles

Tools:

Instead of a large shovel, saw, ax and hammer kit include a garden spade, string saw, and hand ax in a sheath (these are lighter weight and the handle of the hand ax serves as a hammer)

Luxuries:

Camera and film
Binoculars
Journal

During a widespread disaster, additional first-aid supplies might be necessary. Instruction in *Improvised First-Aid Supplies for Emergency Use* tells how to make sterile bandages from sheets and towels. They should be stored with your Home First-Aid Kit.

IMPROVISED FIRST-AID SUPPLIES FOR EMERGENCY USE

You will need: one sheet, single-bed size (approximately 72″×90″); one towel (Turkish type) approximately 26″×46″, or wash cloth to make equal size. Substitute materials may be: baby diapers or baby crib sheets (if no longer needed), large dish towels, sugar sacks, sheeting, or yardage of similar size.

All materials must be freshly laundered and ironed.

Preparation: The following directions are based on the use of one single-bed sized sheet and one medium-sized towel. Smaller quantities can, of course, be obtained from smaller-sized articles.

1. Spread paper on the floor to keep sheet clean; spread sheet on the paper.
2. Measure 36″ from one corner along one side and along one end. Cut or tear square as measured.
3. Fold this square on the bias (corner to the opposite corner) and cut. This will give you two triangular bandages. Fold and put aside.
4. Measure along the side of the remainder of the sheet and mark the following:
   4-3″ strips
   4-4″ strips
   4-6″ strips   If sheet is longer or shorter, adjust accordingly.
5. Tear (or cut) strips across the sheet. They should be approximately 72″ long and used for the larger dressings.

153

6. Take the remainder of the sheet, which will be approximately 32"×36" and measure 2" strips across the short end, so that you will have 2"×36" strips.
7. Tear (or cut) these sixteen 2" strips which are 36" long. You should have the following:

4-6" strips, 72" long   16-2" strips, 36" long
4-4" strips, 72" long   2 triangular bandages
4-3" strips, 72" long

8. From towel cut out the following:

4-6"×24" pieces
4-4"×16" pieces
4-3"×12" pieces

9. Take the 6"×24" pads and fold them twice so that you have 6"×6" squares. Place one of these pads in the center of your 6"×72" strips of sheeting. Sew the lower half of the pad to the sheet, so that the other half may be folded over to make a 6"×6" square or opened along the strip to make a 6"×12" pad.
10. Sew all pads to strips of same size; i.e., the 6" pads on the 6" strips, etc.
11. Cut the cloth so that each size of bandage-compress may be wrapped separately. This will enable you to use some without contaminating the others. The 2"×2" may be wrapped in pairs because of their small size. Paper should be cut so the sides will fold over the bandages and the ends will tuck into each other: about three times the size of the bandage. It is not advisable to use pins, clips, or tape.
12. Plainly mark each package so that you will know what each contains, i.e., 1-6"×6" bandage compress 2-2"×2" bandage compress.

You are now ready to sterilize your materials.

Directions for sterilization have been recommended by the U.S. Health Department.

13. Place the package of compresses in a covered pan. Place in oven. Place another pan in the oven with about 4" of water in it. Set oven for 250°. Thirty minutes from the time water in pan boils, you have completed your sterilization.
14. Use care in removing hot compresses from the pan.
15. Place these packaged compresses in a bag (paper or cloth). Mark the bag: FIRST AID SUPPLIES.

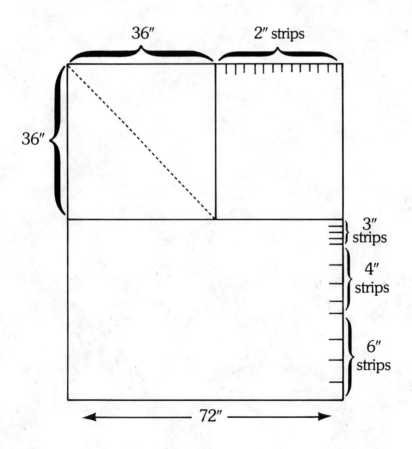

27 BUDGETING

"Almost any man knows how to earn money, but not one in a million knows how to spend it."

Henry David Thoreau

Some say budgeting takes away freedom and ties one down. I believe the opposite. A good budget gives more freedom. It helps decide what's really important and helps us place our priorities, so we can live more abundantly. We become masters over our finances — not the victims. It takes wisdom and skill to spend money wisely and budgeting helps us get the most from our money, *and*, there is satisfaction in exercising discipline over our wants and becoming self sustaining.

As some very wise people have said:

"Dollars go farther when accompanied by sense."

Anonymous

"It is a blessing to not be able to acquire all that we desire."

Brigham Young

"Avoid debt like the plague!"

Brigham Young via my mother
(who is brilliant with a budget!)

"In the old days a man who saved money was a miser: Nowadays he's a wonder."

Anonymous

You too can be a wonder. Work smarter, not harder and have your money working for you. Make a good budget, organize, and become more satisfied with your financial life.

Budgets seem complicated, but if you take this one a step at a time, it's really very simple. Get out a sheet of lined paper and a pencil (you will probably be erasing). Make two columns. In the first column, list everything you have to pay. In the second column list all the things you REALLY want. (We'll come back to the second column later.) There are two types of bills you pay. Some are FIXED expenses (fixed except for inflation): they that are the same, every time you pay them. They might be taxes, church donations, savings, house payments, health and dental insurance, life, car and homeowners insurance, music lessons, sanitation disposal, vacation savings, Christmas savings. Go down your list and write FX by all your fixed expenses. Some you pay every month, some quarterly, some semiannually and annually. Make a note by each and indicate when it has to be paid (M, Q, S, A).

The rest of your bills are FLEXIBLE expenses. These bills vary every time you pay them. Examples might include: Educational expenses, heating, electricity, water, telephone, doctor, dentist, medicines, gas for the car, car repair, entertainment, food, clothing, birthday and gift allowance, house repair, emergencies, and miscellaneous. Some can be paid monthly or at varying times throughout the year. Make a note by each flexible expense (FL) and indicate when it has to be paid.

Now you are ready to fill in the charts on pages 163-165. You may want to reproduce them on lined paper and keep them in a 3 ring binder.

Using Chart #1, record all income. Add the total.

Turn to Chart #2. Starting with monthly, quarterly, semiannual and annual bills, record your Fixed expenses. In the Amount Allowed column, record the amount you pay on your monthly bills. Because you do not pay the other bills monthly, you must compute how much money you need to put aside each month to pay the bill when it comes due. Do this by totaling how much you pay annually and divide by 12. This tells how much you should put aside each month. Enter it in Amount Allowed column.

Using Chart #3, write all your FLEXIBLE expenses beginning with monthly, and so on. In the summer you probably use less heat, electricity, etc. than in the winter. It is important to put extra money aside in the summer to pay for the higher bills in winter. Take an average of all your payments. Figure, by adding together how much you paid each month last year, add 10% to keep up with inflation, and divide by 12. Enter this amount in the Amount Allowed column. For example: Last year for electricity you might have paid $15, $14, $12, $11, $9, $5, $5, $9, $10, $14, $15, $25 from January through December. The total is $144.00. Add 10% for inflation which makes it $159.00 (rounded off). Divide 12 months into $159.00. You get a $14 approximate average. Enter $14.00 across the page as Amount Allowed for electricity.

See Chart #5. As each bill comes in, subtract the bill from the amount allowed. Add the balance to whatever total money has been put aside for electricity. Notice how it equals out over the year.

Because it is the first time to accumulate money, the first year you will need to borrow money from a miscellaneous fund to meet the extra amount during the first few months. After the budget has functioned for a year, you should always have enough money in reserve to meet the bill. The utility company in your area may allow an equal payment for all 12 months. Check with them.

Chart #5

	Jan	Feb	Mar	Apr	May	Jun	Jul	Aug	Sep	Oct	Nov	Dec
Amount Allowed	$14	$14	$14	$14	$14	$14	$14	$14	$14	$14	$14	$14
plus or minus	–	−6	−7	−6	−2	+3	+9	+15	+18	+20	+21	+17
Total	$14	8	7	8	12	17	+23	+29	+32	+34	+35	+31
Amount of Bill	20	15	13	10	9	8	8	11	12	13	18	25
Total carried	−6	−7	−6	−2	+3	+9	+15	+18	+20	+21	+17	+6

The $6 left over in December is carried over to January of the next year.

There are two ways you might handle this accumulated money.

1. You can keep an envelope for each bill. Cash your paycheck at the first of each month, divide the money, putting the specific amount allowed into each envelope. Pay each bill personally as you can't send cash through the mail. Over the summer months, you will accumulate extra money in the envelopes to cover payment of increased bills during winter months. You must not borrow from these envelopes or your budget will not work!

2. With the second method, you put your paycheck in your checking account, and keep track of your money on paper allowing the accumulated money to remain in the bank, drawing interest until you need it to pay the higher bills.

You may want to do this with all the bills you pay only once a month, but for budget items like food, clothing, etc. (items you purchase several times a month) you may want to use the envelope method. Because you spend for these items several times a month, it becomes simpler if you place the money allowed in an envelope designated for that item. If you have money left over at the end of the month, keep it in the envelope and spend it the next month. If you run out before the month is over — quit buying!

You have filled out Chart #1 or your Income Sheet
Chart #2 or your Fixed Expense Sheet
Chart #3 or your Flexible Expense Sheet

You either have money left over or you have problems. Let's examine the problem of not having enough money to go around. There are two choices. 1. You can cut down on spending, meaning you need to analyze where to cut down and streamline. Analyze the things you do, ask yourself, how can I save money? Benjamin Franklin said "Beware of little expenses; a small leak will sink a great ship." Some thoughts you might have are: Don't waste anything, wash dishes by hand, hang out the wash, turn out lights and TV when not in use, turn down the heat, don't waste water, use only what you need of paper toweling, toilet paper, writing paper, food & clothing. Get rid of luxuries you really don't need. Concerning food, fix only what you need, shop wisely and invest only in nourishing foods. Don't go into debt or pay on time. That's like being in bondage.
2. You can increase your income. Many books have been written (you can get them in your library) about thinking positively and increasing your income substantially. If you're a mom and don't want to leave home, think of talents and skills you have that could be marketable. Perhaps you could sew, mend, do washing or ironing, tending children, make crafts and sell them on consignment, fix hair, do painting, calligraphy, wall hangings, grow plants to sell, telephone solicit or type. Have you ever considered teaching? How about specialty cooking, sewing, art, budgeting. Perhaps you could print an advertisement and distribute it or put an ad in the paper. Can you teach piano, guitar, another instrument? Maybe you'd like

to write a book. Children can collect newspapers to recycle, have newspaper routes, sweep sidewalks, mow lawns, trim, cultivate, do housework, wash windows, wash cars, care for someone who is sick, babysit, gather mistletoe from oak trees, bag and sell it for Christmas, pick fruit. Teach children skills, let them help, follow up and support them, reteach with love and patience if necessary.

If you have money left over after deducting your bills from your income, go back to the first sheet of paper, second column. Look over your list of wants and prioritize them. Mark "1" by the one most important to you. Mark each in the order of importance. Now work on a plan to get those things that are the most important. *If* you have money left over, you may buy it. If you don't have money left over, set a goal for yourself as to when you *will* be able to get it. Chart #4 is a goal sheet and will help you organize a plan. Find out how much the item costs. Enter the amount on the goal sheet. Determine how much you have to save for it each month. Compute the number of months it will take to pay for it. Make all the entries on the goal sheet. Every month put that money aside and don't touch it until you reach your goal, then buy it with money in hand. This way you are spending your money on those things really important to you, instead of letting the money slip through your fingers and never getting to the things you most want to do. *Don't* buy on time. Another wise person said, "If you are in debt, someone else owns part of you." And interest is expensive.

As you live and manage your money wisely, there is a sense of enjoyment, satisfaction and accomplishment.

Once you start your budget, stick to it!

Chart #1   Income Sheet

Income Sources	Jan	Feb	Mar	Apr	May	Jun	Jul	Aug	Sep	Oct	Nov	Dec
Total												

Chart #2   Fixed Expense Sheet

	amount allowed	Jan	Feb	Mar	Apr	May	Jun	Jul	Aug	Sep	Oct	Nov	Dec

Chart #3　　Flexible Expense Sheet

Flexible expenses

		Jan	Feb	Mar	Apr	May	Jun	Jul	Aug	Sep	Oct	Nov	Dec
	amount allowed												
	plus or minus												
	total												
	bill												
	total												
	amount allowed												
	plus or minus												
	total												
	bill												
	total												
	amount allowed												
	plus or minus												
	total												
	bill												
	total												
	amount allowed												
	plus or minus												
	total												
	bill												
	total												

Chart #4
Savings for Goals

Goals Being Saved for	Target Date	Budget Period												
		Est Cost	Sav Goal	Act Goal	Sav Goal	Act Goal	Sav Goal	Act Goal	Sav Goal	Act Goal	Sav Goal	Act Goal	Sav Goal	Act Goal
	Total saved													
	Total saved													
	Total saved													
	Total saved													
	Total saved													
	Total saved													
	Total saved													
	Total saved													
	Total saved													
	Total saved													
	Total saved													
	Total Budget													
	Total Actual													

28

READY OR NOT

CHECK LIST

- [ ] You are convinced you should have food storage.
- [ ] You know which foods are good to store.
- [ ] You made a list of what and how much you need.
- [ ] You know where to go for the best buys.
- [ ] You have a plan to finance your storage.
- [ ] You bought your storage and brought it home.
- [ ] You stored it in the right kind of containers and processed it correctly.
- [ ] You stored water.
- [ ] You are keeping records.
- [ ] You arranged an area for food storage.
- [ ] You learned skills for sprouting.
- [ ] You learned to make bread, yogurt, cottage cheese, tofu, etc.
- [ ] You are cooking with your stored food and replenishing your supplies.
- [ ] You know how to cook during an emergency.
- [ ] You have home and car first aid kits and an evacuation kit.
- [ ] You budget your money.
- [ ] You are reaping benefits of physical, emotional and financial security because you are prepared.
- [ ] You've gotten it together and YOU FEEL GREAT!

INDEX